מסורה

# ArtScroll Mesorah Series®

*Expositions on Jewish liturgy and thought*

Rabbis Nosson Scherman / Meir Zlotowitz
*General Editors*

# kaddish

**THE KADDISH PRAYER** / A NEW TRANSLATION
WITH A COMMENTARY ANTHOLOGIZED FROM
TALMUDIC, MIDRASHIC, AND RABBINIC SOURCES.

Published by

Mesorah Publications, ltd

*Translation, Commentary,
and an Overview —
"Kaddish / Prayer of Sanctification"
by*
Rabbi Nosson Scherman

FIRST EDITION
First Impression . . . January 1980
SECOND EDITION
First Impression . . . July 1980
Second Impression . . . November 1982
THIRD EDITION
First Impression . . . October, 1991
Second Impression . . . July 1995
Third Impression . . . October 1997
Fourth Impression . . . October 2001

Published and Distributed by
**MESORAH PUBLICATIONS, Ltd.**
4401 Second Avenue
Brooklyn, New York 11232

Distributed in Europe by
**LEHMANNS**
Unit E, Viking Industrial Park
Rolling Mill Road
Jarrow, Tyne & Wear NE32 3DP
England

Distributed in Australia & New Zealand by
**GOLDS WORLD OF JUDAICA**
3-13 William Street
Balaclava, Melbourne 3183
Victoria Australia

Distributed in Israel by
**SIFRIATI / A. GITLER — BOOKS**
6 Hayarkon Street
Bnei Brak 51127

Distributed in South Africa by
**KOLLEL BOOKSHOP**
Shop 8A Norwood Hypermarket
Norwood 2196, Johannesburg, South Africa

---

### THE ARTSCROLL MESORAH SERIES ®
### KADDISH

---

ISBN
0-89906-160-5 (hard cover)
0-89906-161-3 (paperback)

Typography by Compuscribe at ArtScroll Studios, Ltd.
4401 Second Avenue / Brooklyn, N.Y. 11232 / (718) 921-9000

Printed in the United States of America by Moriah Offset
Bound by Sefercraft, Quality Bookbinders, Ltd. Brooklyn, N.Y.

# ⊷§ Table of Contents

# An Overview —
## Kaddish / Prayer of Sanctification

רַבִּי שִׁמְעוֹן בֶּן גַּמְלִיאֵל אוֹמֵר מִשּׁוּם רַבִּי יְהוֹשֻׁעַ
מִיּוֹם שֶׁחָרַב בֵּית הַמִּקְדָּשׁ אֵין יוֹם שֶׁאֵין בּוֹ קְלָלָה
וְלֹא יָרַד הַטַּל לִבְרָכָה וְנִיטַּל טַעַם הַפֵּירוֹת. אָמַר
רָבָא בְּכָל יוֹם וָיוֹם מְרֻבָּה קִלְלָתוֹ מִשֶּׁל חֲבֵרוֹ ...
וְאֶלָּא עָלְמָא אַמַּאי קָא מְקַיֵּם? אַקְּדוּשָׁה דְסִדְרָא
וְאִיהֵא שְׁמֵהּ רַבָּא דְּאַגַּדְתָּא

R' Shimon ben Gameliel said on behalf of
R' Yehoshua: From the day He destroyed
the Holy Temple, there is no day without
curse, the dewfall was not blessed, and the
[delicious] taste was removed from crops.
Rava said: Each new day the curse is
greater than that of the day before ... In
what merit, then, does the world survive?
— Because of Kedushah D'Sidra [the
recitation of the angelic declaration 'Holy,
Holy, Holy' during the U'Va L'Zion
prayer] and Yehei Shmei Rabbah [in the
Kaddish] following the public study of
Aggadah (Sotah 48a, 49a).

# I. May His Great Name Be Blessed

*Two
Prayers*

**K**addish has become one of the most familiar
words in the vocabulary of Jews. Whether in
harsh lands where the ravages of oppression have
been heaviest or in hospitable countries where the
smiles of opportunity have conquered more Jewish

*The name Kaddish
has evoked Jewish
feeling and
reawakened filial
sensitivities that
lay dormant in the
face of all else.*

souls than whips and dungeons, the name *Kaddish*
has evoked Jewish feeling and reawakened filial sensitivities that lay dormant in the face of all else. For is
not *Kaddish* the prayer for the dead? And breathes
there a son or daughter who could stand at the bier of

a parent without at least a twinge of remorse for duty unfulfilled? Is there a human being too insecure and too busy to relax his pursuit of a relentless future — at least once a year — and look back at those whose toil formed his past?

With such emotions has *Kaddish* been described, honored, and recited — and misunderstood.

*Kaddish contains no mention of death or guilt or nostalgia. Rather it is a declaration of faith in Israel's national purpose.*

For *Kaddish* contains no mention of death or guilt or nostalgia. Rather it is a declaration of faith in Israel's national purpose, of loyalty to Israel's Creator, of confidence in the ultimate triumph of the ideals for which heaven and earth were created, of longing for the time when people — *all* people — will accept the Heavenly mission that gives meaning to life and transcends death, that will illuminate the darkest moments of personal and universal tragedy. [See *commentary* to stich 1 of *Kaddish*.] Such an expression gives hope and direction to life and striving. Indeed, as mankind grows increasingly oblivious of the sanctity represented by the ideals of the Holy Temple, the universe owes its very survival to Jews who — whether in large, secure multitudes or fearful, huddled groups — have historically braved every circumstance to raise their voices in the central theme of *Kaddish*:

יְהֵא שְׁמֵהּ רַבָּא מְבָרַךְ לְעָלַם וּלְעָלְמֵי עָלְמַיָּא
*May His great Name be blessed forever and ever.*

Let us attempt to understand the secret of this seven-word, twenty-eight-letter proclamation and the *Kaddish* that is built around it.

*Why is it so potent that when God hears us reciting it, He grieves over the destruction of Jerusalem and likens Himself to a father who forced his son into exile?*

Why is it so potent that when God hears us reciting it, He grieves over the destruction of Jerusalem and likens Himself to a father who forced his son into exile (*Berachos* 3a)? And what is there about a recitation of *Amen Yehei Shmei Rabbah* with all one's strength [בְּכָל כֹּחוֹ] that can cause the gates of Paradise [גַּן עֵדֶן] to open wide and to annul even a decree of lifetime-long suffering (*Shabbos* 119a)? And what is the common denominator of *Amen Yehei Shmei Rabbah* and *Kedushah D'Sidra* [the Hebrew-Aramaic narrative of the angels' praises] that is potent enough to guarantee the continued existence of the universe (*Sotah* 49a)?

## To Sanctify The Name

כָּל בֵּית יִשְׂרָאֵל מְצֻוִּין עַל קִדּוּשׁ הַשֵּׁם הַגָּדוֹל הַזֶּה שֶׁנֶּאֱמַר, וְנִקְדַּשְׁתִּי בְּתוֹךְ בְּנֵי יִשְׂרָאֵל

*The entire Family of Israel is commanded concerning the Sanctification of this Great Name, as it is written [Leviticus 22:32]: And I shall be sanctified amid the children of Israel (Rambam, Hilchos Yesodei HaTorah 5:1).*

*One of the first commandments listed by Rambam in Mishneh Torah is the responsibility to sanctify God's Name.* One of the first commandments listed by *Rambam* in *Mishneh Torah*, his monumental compendium of Torah law, is the responsibility incumbent upon the entire Jewish nation — not merely its scholars, leaders, and people of influence — to sanctify God's Name. Indeed, this was the purpose of creation, that it serve as a vehicle to demonstrate the greatness of its Creator until all the universe would recognize and proclaim that God is One and His Name is One [see *commentary* to stich 1 of *Kaddish*].

*Sanctification of God's Name has nothing to do with satisfying public opinion. There is only one Jewish definition of the term: To live according to God's dictates in letter and spirit.* Sanctification of God's Name has nothing to do with satisfying public opinion. There is only one Jewish definition of the term: To live according to God's dictates in letter and spirit. If the result is ridicule, then the Jew must be buoyed by the conviction that, in the words of *R' Yonah*, it is better to be mocked for an entire lifetime on earth, than to be mocked by God for even an instant in the World to Come.

*The lonely Jew who defies taunt and contempt to serve God has sanctified His Name infinitely more than a multitude of compromisers who bend and sway at every frown and sneer.* If such behavior earns one the respect and even the emulation of his neighbors, so much the better. But God requires no mass approval to satisfy Him; the lonely Jew who defies taunt and contempt to serve God has sanctified His Name infinitely more than a multitude of compromisers who bend and sway at every frown and sneer.

*Meshech Chochmah* (*Leviticus* 19:2) describes such sanctification in poetic, but scrupulously halachic, terms:

God is infinite. He requires no perfection beyond His own ... But because of His abundant kindness, He created a universe with countless, lofty spheres all of which recount His glory and comprehend their exalted Creator. Within this vast universe, He created one small dot, a crude and material thing, tiny and insignificant in the scheme of the cosmos — planet Earth. In it are thousands of species. Among them is one puny, base, weakly constituted creature, nearly three cubits tall ... an untamed ruffian with no inherent knowledge or comprehension of his Maker and Guide. He is filled with contradictions: corruption and righteousness, evil and good, foolishness and wisdom, ugliness and beauty, sloth and alacrity, and so on by the countless thousands ... He is truly a miniature universe — and he can utilize this quality for limitless good ... or evil.

> *Among them is one puny, base, weakly constituted creature, nearly three cubits tall ... an untamed ruffian with no inherent knowledge or comprehension of his Maker.*

The first [to realize his potential to scale spiritual heights] was Abraham ... and after him, Isaac and Jacob ... God chose their offspring, inspired them to perceive Him and gave them of His sublime wisdom — the Torah — by means of which they could utilize every material thing for His service. The Jew does his Maker's will on earth, if he dedicates everything to Him — for the dedication of oneself and his fortune to God, Blessed be He, is the primary form of sanctification — his body to serve and revere Him, his heart and intellect to love Him, to bring his servants, family, and loved ones nearer to His service. When the earth is abloom and its flowers are blossoming, the sound of Torah will be heard and the exultation of the Lord will fill the world — the bringers of *Bikkurim* [First Fruits] will sing beautifully, separate their tithes, and have them given to those who sing the songs of praise in the Temple of God ... As the *Mechilta* teaches, there is no thing and no activity on earth that cannot be utilized to serve God ...

> *When the earth is abloom and its flowers are blossoming, the sound of Torah will be heard and the exultation of the Lord will fill the world.*

This is the uniquely human variety of holiness. It does not suggest freedom from temptation and contradictory urges, it does not negate the satisfaction of physical needs or toil in field and workshop. Only angels have such freedom — but angels lack the greatness that comes with facing challenges and overcoming them. An angel cannot create the sanc-

*An angel cannot create the sanctification that comes with making each crop, commission, and salary a vehicle for using property as the Torah directs.* tification that comes with making each crop, commission, and salary a vehicle for using property as the Torah directs. Only man can so regulate behavior and sublimate reactions, that he transforms the 'puny, base, three-cubit ruffian' into the finished image of God for whose sake heaven and earth were created.

## Man Above Angel

Still, an angel is closer to sanctity because he is not subject to the frailty and temptation of physical existence. The angels praise God with the cry of

קָדוֹשׁ קָדוֹשׁ קָדוֹשׁ ה׳ צְבָאוֹת מְלֹא כָל הָאָרֶץ כְּבוֹדוֹ

*Holy, Holy, Holy is HASHEM of hosts — all the world is filled with His glory (Isaiah 6:3).*

We echo their praise in our own prayers. In בִּרְכוֹת קְרִיאַת שְׁמַע, the *Blessings of the Shema*, and the *Kedushah* of the *chazzan's Shemoneh Esrei*, we say with the angels that God is triply holy. In *Kedushah* we rise to our feet and lift our heels from the ground to symbolize an awareness that these perceptions of God's holiness truly raise us from the grip of earth's coarseness *(Maharal)* — we say it, we know it to be true, but we are only echoing the angels. God wants more of us. Indeed, He wants more than the angels can offer Him. For theirs is a perception of holiness that is ingrained, not acquired; an awareness that was given, not gained by hard-fought effort.

*We lift our heels from the ground to symbolize an awareness that these perceptions of God's holiness truly raise us from the grip of earth's coarseness.*

In *Kedushah D'Sidra*, the daily repetition of these angelic praises during the *U'Va L'Zion* prayer, there is a difference. True, we again repeat the litany of the angels, but now it becomes our *own*, *human* perception of God's sanctity. Admittedly our comprehension of Him is inferior to that of the angels, but it means more to God because it is ours. That is why *U'Va L'Zion* translates these *praises* into Aramaic, the language of the masses. [The significance of Aramaic will be discussed below.] Two different, but

*Admittedly our comprehension of Him is inferior to that of the angels, but it means more to God because it is ours.*

similar interpretations of *Kedushah D'Sidra* are the following:

(A) The *Kedushah* of the angels represents the holiness which sustained creation while the Holy Temple stood. Then, God's life-giving influence was channeled to earth through His Sanctuary in Jerusalem. Then, holiness was more pervasive, more apparent, more recognizable than it has been in times since. Even with the destruction of the Temple, however, God's sustenance did not cease; were that ever to happen the universe could no longer exist. There is still a flow of spiritual nourishment, but now it comes through Israel, and because of the sanctity created by its individual members. The blessings are not nearly as abundant as they were when the Temple stood — the Sages teach that even fruits do not taste as delicious, a mere indication of how diminished the universe becomes in the absence of the Temple — but still, God does not forsake His creatures. He continues to breathe life into them and their world, but to a reduced degree. We symbolize this lesser degree of Divine influence by expressing our perception of God's holiness in Aramaic, a language with far less holiness than Hebrew (see *Maharal: Nesiv HaAvodah* 11; *Gevuros Hashem* ch. 54; *Chiddushei Aggados, Shabbos* 12b and *Sotah* 33b).

*The Sages teach that even fruits do not taste as delicious; a mere indication of how diminished the universe becomes in the absence of the Temple — but still, God does not forsake His creatures.*

(B) In *Kedushah D'Sidrah* our repetition of the Holy, Holy, Holy praises are introduced with וְאַתָּה קָדוֹשׁ יוֹשֵׁב תְּהִלּוֹת יִשְׂרָאֵל, *Yet You are the Holy One, enthroned upon the praises of Israel* (Psalms 22:4). This is the introduction to the praises that are to follow: No matter how exalted God is, He is enthroned upon *our* praises. What *we* say means more to Him than the loftiest expressions of the angels. Although we will quote the angels, we will translate their words into *our* language as *we* perceive Him in our own imperfect, human way. Though we are limited by our humanness, our achievements are precious to God because they are *achievements*, not Heavenly gifts. He is King because — and to the extent that —

*No matter how exalted God is, He is enthroned upon our praises. What we say means more to Him than the loftiest expressions of the angels.*

we proclaim Him King *(Meshech Chochmah).*

It is instructive to study the Sages' Aramaic translation of God's triple degree of holiness:

*He is holy in His lofty heaven above, abode of His Presence; He is holy on earth where He works His mighty deeds; He is holy* [וּלְעָלַם וּלְעָלְמֵי עָלְמַיָּא] *forever and ever.* Maharal comments that only two times in our entire order of prayers do we use that last expression — in *Kedushah D'Sidra* and in the *Yehei Shmei Rabbah* of *Kaddish.* This is no insignificant coincidence; let us remember the Sages teaching that the universe remains in existence only because of these two prayers. This unique expression, which means literally *to the world and all worlds of the world,* signifies the concept that God's life-giving power flows from the very highest degree of holiness — from His Own Presence — down to the flesh-and-blood, cause-and-effect world in which we human beings live. [See commentary to stich 4, especially footnote outlining the interpretation of *Nefesh HaChaim* which sheds much light on this concept.]

*Only two times in our entire order of prayers do we use that last expression: in Kedushah D'Sidra and in the Yehei Shmei Rabbah of Kaddish.*

But there is another vital key to our understanding of these two supports of our existence. Let us note that the Talmud speaks of one *Yehei Shmei Rabbah* in particular — יְהֵא שְׁמֵהּ רַבָּא דְּאַגַּדְתָּא, *the Yehei Shmei Rabbah recited after the public study of Aggadah.*

*Rashi (Sotah* 49a) explains that *Kedushah D'Sidra* and public Torah study have one key aspect in common. The Sages instituted *Kedushah D'Sidra* as a combination of the Scriptural verses and their translation in the vernacular so that all people would engage in at least that minimum amount of Torah study every day. The combination of this declaration of God's holiness with the public study of Torah gives this prayer special efficacy. Similarly, there is great merit in the Sabbath custom of gathering the populace to hear sages teach the Torah, and concluding that study session with a recitation of *Kaddish,* a proclamation of God's holiness.

*The combination of this declaration of God's holiness with the public study of Torah gives this prayer special efficacy.*

Torah is our gift from the highest of worlds; it is God's own wisdom expressed in human terms. The Holy Temple is gone, but Torah remains and Israel's public acknowledgment of God's holiness remains — so creation survives.

# II. Yehei Shmei Rabbah

*Roots Above*

Like so many verses of Scripture and texts of the liturgy, the number of words and letters in the various parts of the *Kaddish* contains allusions which are in addition to the simple and deeper meanings of the texts. [See commentary to stiches 6 and 7 of *Kaddish* for such numerical allusions.] One such verse is *Yehei Shmei Rabbah.* As the commentary will explain, the stich contains seven words that are accompanied by an eighth, the *Amen* that precedes it.

*In God's scheme of creation, 'seven' represents a form of completion.*

Maharal, R' Hirsch and many other commentators note that in God's scheme of creation the number seven represents a form of completion. There are seven days in the week, seven years in a *shmittah* [Sabbatical-year] cycle, seven weeks of preparation from the Exodus until the giving of Ten Commandments on Mount Sinai, seven Kabbalistic *sefiros* [spiritual stages of development from the time an idea is born until it takes final shape and becomes an accomplished fact].

*Sometimes, an earthly fact has roots and effects that transcend the earthly setting where it takes place.*

Sometimes, an earthly fact has roots and effects that transcend the earthly setting where it takes place. Abraham's circumcision of himself, for example, involved a man, a knife, and an operation that has been repeated many millions of times since. But his circumcision clearly transcended any physical act that had ever taken place before. His act sealed the covenant between God and Israel; it tied God and His People to one another for all time in a bond that cannot be severed. As such, it was a physical act with cosmic implications. Such a higher realm of deed is symbolized by the number eight. A boy waits seven days from his birth, on the *eighth* day — after the

*Such a higher realm of deed is symbolized by the number eight. A boy waits seven days from his birth, on the eighth day he is circumcised.*

earthly seven-day cycle is completed — he is circumcised, to symbolize that his circumcision, like Abraham's, has effects that go beyond the laws of nature and physics.

## Opening the Gates

As a seven-word formula, *Yehei Shmei Rabbah* is an expression of total dedication. But it begins with an *eighth* word, *Amen.* The total formula expresses the idea that this eight-word response has cosmic implications far beyond the comprehension of anyone who has ever proclaimed it. The same holds true for the eight words of praise in *Kaddish* that follow *Yehei Shmei Rabbah* [see commentary to stich 7]: God's praises go infinitely beyond human understanding, and a proclamation of His boundless greatness contributes to the Sanctification of His Name to a degree we can never even hope to perceive (*Nesiv HaAvodah* 11).

*God's praises go infinitely beyond human understanding, and a proclamation of His boundless greatness contributes to the Sanctification of His Name.*

The *Zohar* (*Terumah*) teaches that *Yehei Shmei Rabbah* has enormous spiritual power, far beyond that of any other acknowledgment of God's holiness. Recited with proper concentration and vigor, it can destroy evil forces that result from man's misdeeds and prevent God's splendor from being revealed to His children. Thus, it was composed in Aramaic, a language that lacks the holiness of Hebrew and is therefore utilized by the forces of evil. By exalting God in Aramaic, we bring holiness to the dark corners of earth where it could not otherwise penetrate.*

*By exalting God in Aramaic we bring holiness to the dark corners of earth where it could not otherwise penetrate.*

Because of the awesome quality inherent in *Yehei Shmei Rabbah*, ARIzal urged that it should be recited with an inner resolve to accept even martyrdom for the sake of God. When a Jew says these words with such feeling, God's Name is sanctified beyond imagination. We cannot even dream of the good that the one verse of praise can accomplish. Small wonder, therefore, that *Zohar* refers to *Yehei Shmei Rabbah* as a *Kedushah*, the same title that is given to

---

* Concerning the matter of the Aramaic language in prayer, see *Berachos* 3a, *Shabbos* 12b, and *Sotah* 33b with *Tosafos* and other commentators. See also *Bais Yosef Orach Chaim* 101 and *Shulchan Aruch, O.Ch.* 101:4.

the sublime song of the angels! (*Yesod V'Shoresh HaAvodah*).

אָמַר רֵישׁ לָקִישׁ כָּל הָעוֹנֶה אָמֵן בְּכָל כֹּחוֹ פּוֹתְחִין לוֹ שַׁעֲרֵי גַן עֵדֶן ... מַאי אָמֵן? אֵל מֶלֶךְ נֶאֱמָן

*Reish Lakish said: Anyone who answers Amen with all his strength — they open the gates of Paradise for him ... What is Amen? [It forms the acronym of]* God the faithful King *(Shabbos 119b).*

*The closed gates of Paradise do not swing open easily, because no one can enter unless he is worthy.*

The closed gates of Paradise do not swing open easily, because no one can enter unless he is worthy — and who can say he is deserving of the ultimate spiritual reward? Yet, *Reish Lakish* tells us that for responding *Amen* with *all his strength*, a person can not only enter gates that remain sealed in the face of many other good deeds — the heavenly forces will rush with alacrity to clear the way for him. *Reish Lakish* does not even mention the one who recites the blessing to which the *Amen* response is made. For, as the Talmud (*Berachos 53b*) teaches, גָּדוֹל הָעוֹנֶה אָמֵן יוֹתֵר מִן הַמְּבָרֵךְ, *He who responds Amen is greater than he who recited the blessing* [*to which the response is made*]. The mystery is now even greater — why is the response great enough to earn entry into Paradise and why is it greater than a blessing?

*Why is the response great enough to earn entry into Paradise, and why is it greater than a blessing?*

R' Bachya (*Kad HaKemach*) comments, as do others, that the word *Amen* is derived from the same root as *Emunah* [faith]. By responding *Amen* to another's blessing, a Jew affirms that he believes in the statement that has been made. By his assent he gives the statement a greater degree of force, for when an individual testifies to God's power by blessing Him for one of His manifestations — the God Who gives bread, heals the sick, heeds prayer, or whatever — he is like a single witness making a statement. When a listener responds *Amen*, he seconds the statement of praise. Now there are *two* witnesses testifying to the statement, and it has far more force and standing. Therefore, the one who responds is greater than the one who prompted him, because the second gave effect to the statement of the first.

*When a listener responds Amen, he seconds the statement of praise. Now there are two witnesses.*

**Superiority of Amen**

*Maharal* offers another insight. A blessing *should*, of course, be recited with proper בַּוָּנָה, *intent, understanding, and concentration*. Yet any prayer composed by the Sages has such holiness by virtue of the *Ruach HaKodesh* [Holy Spirit] with which it was formulated, that it has significant efficacy even when its recitation is perfunctory. True, one who *does* have proper intent, rises above the minimum level, but he is still reciting a prayer which, by its very nature, is not dependent on his inner feeling for its effectiveness. His own person does not create the blessing; the Sages have done that. But *Amen* is entirely different. By definition, *Amen* is a personal affirmation. In effect, the listener says, 'You are reciting the words of a formula taught us by the Sages, but *I*, in the innermost recesses of my being, *know* that it is true. You recite and I *affirm*. You repeat and I *believe*.'

*Amen is a personal affirmation. In effect, the listener says, 'You are reciting the words of a formula taught us by the Sages, but I know that it is true.'*

A blessing can be a blessing — albeit an imperfect one — even without intent, but a perfunctory *Amen* is totally worthless. *Bais Yosef (O.Ch. 56)* goes so far as to say that a mindless *Amen* is meaningless and may as well *not have been said*, a view that *Aruch HaShulchan* cites in 56:5.

Seen in this light, a proper *Amen* is indeed worthier than a blessing. It has to be, because it demands more of the person reciting it. Such an *Amen* can indeed open the gates of Paradise. But it must be בְּכָל כֹּחוֹ, *with all his strength*. Most commentators interpret this either literally: in a loud, strong voice; or figuratively: with the inner strength of intent and concentration. (See commentary to stich 6.)

*Maharal* interprets differently:

*Since Amen represents deep, uncompromising faith in God, it is the voice of the soul overpowering the unwilling body.*

Since *Amen* represents deep, uncompromising faith in God, it is the voice of the soul overpowering the unwilling body. The animal in man would prefer not to believe, not to deny his lust and subdue his passion. When the soul triumphs and wrests a sincere *Amen* out of a reluctant mouth, the body-soul combination that is man has ascended a rung on the ladder from earth to heaven. This does not require shouting, nor need we be *told* that it requires concentration, for *Amen*, by definition, *is* concentration. Rather the requirement is that it be enunciated clearly and perfectly, not in a semi-articulate mumble. Thus recited, the *Amen* provides the two characteristics that earn entry into Paradise:

(A) The clear enunciation symbolizes opening of the gates. Just as one cannot enter Paradise if its gates remain closed, so the *Amen* that gains him entry should be articulated clearly by the previously immobile organs of speech.

*Just as one cannot enter Paradise if its gates remain closed, so the Amen that gains him entry should be articulated clearly.*

(B) More importantly, by answering *Amen* inwardly as well as outwardly, a Jew demonstrates that he has broken the shackles of his material existence and entered a better, higher world. *Amen* is in his heart, not merely in his mouth. He may walk, work, eat, and sleep on earth, but in his intellect and emotions, he is *already* in a better, higher world. Therefore, the gates of Paradise swing open and the angels step forward to greet him.

*Amen is in his heart, in his intellect and emotions, he is already in a better, higher world.*

What glorious opportunities! If only there were one *Yehei Shmei Rabbah* a year and one *Amen* a season. Knowing that these are the keys to holiness and Paradise, we would prepare for them far in advance, as befits such momentous occasions. We would respond to the *chazzan* with an inner and outer crescendo of feeling and sound. We would almost see the gates of Paradise open before our mind's eye.

*If only there were one Yehei Shmei Rabbah a year, we would respond to the chazzan with an inner and outer crescendo of feeling and sound.*

But there are scores of *Amens* to say every day and as many as a dozen or more recitations of *Kaddish* to hear. *Amen* becomes a habit, *Yehei Shmei Rabbah* an intrusion. Lips become trained to answer when minds are continents away.

May the lessons of the Sages become part of us so that our responses may assure life to the universe, and afterlife to ourselves.

# III. The Mourner's Kaddish

„כַּפֵּר לְעַמְּךָ יִשְׂרָאֵל אֲשֶׁר פָּדִיתָ". דָּרְשׁוּ בַּפְּסִיקְתָּא... אֵלּוּ הַמֵּתִים שֶׁמִּתְכַּפְּרִין בְּמָמוֹן הַחַיִּים. וְלָמַדְנוּ מִזֶּה שֶׁהַהַקְדָּשׁוֹת שֶׁנּוֹהֲגִין הַחַיִּים לְהַקְדִּישָׁם בְּעַד הַמֵּתִים שֶׁיֵּשׁ לָהֶם תּוֹעֶלֶת לַמֵּתִים... וְהוּא הַדִּין לְאוֹמֵר בִּשְׁבִילוֹ קַדִּישׁ אוֹ שׁוּם בְּרָכָה בְּבֵית הַכְּנֶסֶת בְּצִבּוּר כְּמוֹ... בְּמַעֲשֶׂה שֶׁל רַבִּי עֲקִיבָא

Absolve Your nation Israel which you redeemed (Deut. *21:8*). *The Rabbis expounded in the Pesikta, '... this refers to the dead who can receive atonement through the charity of the living.' From this we learn that the dead derive benefit from charity which the living sanctify in their behalf... This also applies to one who recites Kaddish or any blessing publicly in the synagogue as... in the story of R' Akiva (R' Bachya, Deut. 21:6).*

*Still Fruitful Deeds*

People are judged for what they did, but they are also judged for what they caused. The person who contributed money, energy, or inspiration to a yeshivah is rewarded for his generosity. He has given of his resources and of himself to do the will of God and help others. That is true, yet it is only part of the story, for the benefits of his concern do not stop with the receipt and handshake. The institution he helped will go on to shape people and help form a generation, perhaps many generations. Does not the investor in a new business continue to draw dividends for as long as the firm thrives? Should not the contributor to a worthy cause continue to earn a reward for as long as his gesture bears fruit?

*Should not the contributor to a worthy cause continue to earn a reward for as long as his gesture bears fruit?*

And what of the further effects of his deed? People were affected for the better by the fact that there existed a school for them to attend. They were molded by the Torah they studied there, the values they absorbed there. Their families, friends, neighbors, children — everything and everyone they touched — were made better to some degree because a yeshivah existed to bring its students closer to the will of God. Even the most sophisticated computer cannot determine how much each individual will share in the beneficial results of the countless efforts in which he had a hand. But God knows.

*Even the most sophisticated computer cannot determine how much each individual must share in the beneficial results of each of countless efforts in which he had a hand.*

There were parents who removed their telephones and skipped lunches during the Great Depression of 1929 so that they could continue paying meager yeshiva tuitions for their children. Who but God can evaluate such deeds? Probably no institution was spared bankruptcy by their sacrifice, but it surely helped. Some of their grandchildren and great-grandchildren are now Torah scholars, teachers, and community leaders, because "insignificant" people more than half-a-century ago refused the entice-ments of tuition-free public schools. Even those who may have drifted away from Judaism, might still re-tain concern for their fellow Jews, and within them are dormant, but still alive, sparks of regard for holy causes and Jewish eternity.

Those parents may now be in a world where the cost of telephones and lunches is of no account. It is a world where a Heavenly Accountant measures the deeds they accomplished in life — and notes also the existence and contributions of many future genera-tions that live fruitfully and productively as Jews, in part because of little things that no human mind could ever evaluate, or even know.

*God never closes the books on a life as long as the ripples of that life are still moving and churning.*

God never closes the books on a life as long as the ripples of that life are still moving and churning. This is the meaning of the *Pesikta's* statement that the dead can receive atonement through the charity of the living. True, the Heavenly accounts of reward and punishment, *mitzvah* and sin, are limited to the deeds of the lone individual being judged. But, in far more than a symbolic sense, the deeds of the living are those of the departed.

*But in far more than a symbolic sense, the deeds of the living are those of the departed.*

The child who contributes to charity in memory of

a parent, the descendant whose heart is warm and hand is open because of the spiritual legacy of ancestors he never knew — these are truly part of the spiritual treasury of the departed. Such deeds occurred because of Jewish fathers whose determination surmounted hardship and ridicule, because of Jewish mothers whose faith and warmth overcame bare cupboards and enticing futures for their children, because of deeds that seemed to be instinctive and natural and unimportant and quixotic and impractical and forgotten as soon as they were done — yet could not be buried by the sands of time. God knows and notes them in His ledger. So the dead find atonement in deeds they never contemplated, but that are nevertheless theirs.

*God knows and notes them in His ledger. So the dead find atonement in deeds they never contemplated, but that are nevertheless theirs.*

So it is, *R' Bachya* continues, with one who recites *Kaddish* in the synagogue. *Kaddish* is a public declaration that God's Name will be sanctified. That Jews long for that time and proclaim their confidence that it will come is in itself an act of sanctification. Rational people have wondered for centuries why Israel does not resign itself to the disappearance decreed for us by all the laws of history. We do not disappear. We do not even 'resign ourselves to our fate,' whatever that means. We confidently predict that God's Name will yet be exalted and sanctified, blessed and praised — by *everyone*, even those who presently deny Him most vehemently.

*R' Chaim ben Bezalel (Sefer HaChaim)* detects a deeper significance in the *Kaddish* of a mourner. A parent has been taken from him; who could blame a child for complaining, at least inwardly, that the loss came too soon, or was preceded by too much suffering, or that the years on earth could have been happier, easier, more successful? Instead, the survivor stands amid his peers and announces, *Yisgadal v'yiskadash Shmei Rabbah... Yehei shmei rabbah m'vorach l'olam ul'olmei olmaya... May His great Name be exalted and sanctified ... May His great Name be blessed forever and ever.* God is just and His ways are just. Though we may not understand

*Who could blame a child for complaining that the loss came too soon, or was preceded by too much suffering, or that the years on earth could have been happier, easier, more successful?*

why death was so quick or life less sweet, we acknowledge that God is just. In effect we say, 'I am comforted over the loss of my earthly parent because his fate is a manifestation of the will of my Father in Heaven, His *just* Will, and thereby my parent's end and my acceptance of it are a Sanctification of the Name.' So the dead find atonement through their living heirs.

## Rabbi Akiva's Compassion

As R' Bachya concludes, the basis for this universal custom of reciting *Kaddish* is the story of R' Akiva.*

*Once, R' Akiva saw a bizarre man with a complexion black as coal.*

Once, R' Akiva saw a bizarre man with a complexion black as coal. On his head, he was carrying a load heavy enough for ten men, and he was running swiftly as a horse. R' Akiva ordered him to stop.

'Why do you do such hard work?,' the Tanna asked.

The apparition answered, 'Do not detain me lest my supervisors be angry with me.'

'What is this? What do you do?'

'I am a dead man,' he replied. 'Every day I am punished anew by being sent to chop wood for a fire in which I am consumed.'

'What did you do in life, my son?' asked R' Akiva.

'I was a tax-collector. I would be lenient with the rich and oppress the poor.'

R' Akiva persisted. 'Have you heard if there is any way to save you?'

'I heard that if only I had left a son who would stand before the congregation and call out בָּרְכוּ אֶת ה' הַמְבֹרָךְ, *Bless HASHEM, Who is to be blessed* — to which the people would respond בָּרוּךְ ה' הַמְבֹרָךְ לְעֹלָם וָעֶד, *Blessed is HASHEM, Who is to be blessed, forever and ever!* And if only had I left a son who could proclaim to the congregation, יִתְגַּדַּל וְיִתְקַדַּשׁ שְׁמֵהּ רַבָּא, *May His great Name be exalted and sanctified* — to which the people would respond יְהֵא שְׁמֵהּ רַבָּא מְבָרַךְ..., *May His great Name be blessed!* If I had such a son I would be released from my punishment.

*And if only had I left a son who could proclaim to the congregation, 'May His great Name be exalted and sanctified!'*

* We give the familiar version found in *Or Zarua*, although the story is also cited, with slight variations in *Menoras HaMaor* (Ner 1, 1:1) who quotes one version from *Midrash Tanchuma, Noach* and another from *Maseches Kallah*. *Eliyahu Zuta* (ch. 17) cites a similar story that occurred with R' Yochanan ben Zakkai.

But I left no son ... When I died, my wife was pregnant, but even if she had a son, there would be no one to teach him.

That moment R' Akiva resolved to discover if a boy had been born and, if so, to teach him until he could lead the congregation in prayer. He went to Ludkia and inquired after the despised tax-collector. 'May the bones of the wicked one be pulverized!' the people spat out. To R' Akiva's inquiries about the widow, they responded, 'May her memory be obliterated from the earth!' And his child — 'He is not even circumcised.'

R' Akiva took the child, had him circumcised, and personally taught him Torah and the order of prayers. When he was ready, R' Akiva appointed him to lead the congregation in prayer.

'Bor'chu es HASHEM...' and the people blessed Him. 'Yisgadal V'yiskadash shmei rabbah...' and the people responded, 'Yehei shmei rabbah...'

Instantly the tortured soul was freed from its punishment. That very night, it appeared to R' Akiva in a dream and blessed him. 'May it be God's will that your mind be at ease in Paradise, for You have rescued me from the judgment of Gehinnom.'

R' Akiva cried out to God, 'May you be known as HASHEM [the Attribute of Mercy] forever; HASHEM is Your appellation throughout the generations!'

## From Jacob's Day

Although the custom for mourners to recite Kaddish began in the Middle Ages, we have seen above (part I) that the effect of Kaddish was well known in the time of the Talmud. What happened in medieval times was only that the collective spiritual genius of Israel used the earlier teachings as the basis for the universal custom to recite Kaddish as a source of merit for the departed soul. At the very birth of the nation we find that the total submission to God's will and the goal of universal sanctification on the part of surviving children brings fulfillment to the soul of a departing parent.

The Sages teach that Jacob, on his deathbed, wished to reveal to his children everything destined to befall the nation, but the spirit of prophecy left

*R' Akiva took the child, had him circumcised, and personally taught him Torah and the order of prayers.*

*The tortured soul was freed from its punishment.*

*The Sages teach that Jacob, on his deathbed, wished to reveal to his children everything destined to befall the nation, but the spirit of prophecy left him.*

him, and with it the secrets he was prepared to im-
part. He was afraid — why had this happened? Could
it be that one or more of his sons was unworthy, that
his lifetime of spiritual toil to produce the perfect
family had ended in failure?

His children reassured him saying שְׁמַע יִשְׂרָאֵל ה'
אֱלֹהֵינוּ ה' אֶחָד, *Hear O Israel* [our father, i.e., they ad-
dressed him by his name, Israel] — HASHEM *our*
*God, HASHEM is One.* They testified that no doubt
or weakness had entered their hearts or diluted their
faith. God's reason for denying them knowledge of
the future was not because they lacked faith in Him
ח"ו to even the slightest degree. Jacob responded
with relief and gratitude בָּרוּךְ שֵׁם כְּבוֹד מַלְכוּתוֹ לְעוֹלָם
וָעֶד, *Blessed is the name of His glorious kingdom*
*forever,* a prayer we retain in our recitation of the
*Shema.*

In describing this event, *Targum Yerushalmi*
states that Jacob's response was יְהֵא שְׁמֵהּ רַבָּא מְבָרַךְ
לְעָלְמֵי עָלְמִין, *May His great Name be blessed forever,*
with only the slightest variation that is the major
congregational response in *Kaddish.* It is clear that
*Targum Yerushalmi* equates the communal response
in *Kaddish* with that of *Shema (Avodas Yisrael; Iyun*
*Tefillah).* Without a doubt, the untarnished righteousness of Jacob's entire family represented a *Kid-*
*dush Hashem* [Sanctification of God's Name] of
enormous proportions. It was that sanctification
which comforted Jacob and made him confident that
his life's purpose had been fulfilled. He expressed his
sense of vindication and fulfillment with the central
theme of *Kaddish* — the same theme that his descen-
dants would adopt nearly three thousand years later
as an orphan's way to gain heavenly peace for the
soul of a departed parent.

R' Simchah Bunam of P'shis'cha adds another insight into the *Kaddish* custom. That mourners
proclaim the longing for sanctification points up the
significance of even a *single* Jewish soul in God's
scheme for the universe. In a human army, the loss
of a single soldier goes completely unnoticed. When

*Targum*
*Yerushalmi*
*equates the*
*communal*
*response in*
*Kaddish with that*
*of Shema.*

hundreds or thousands of soldiers are lost, a void is felt and new recruits must be conscripted, otherwise the plans of the state cannot be carried out properly; but an individual soldier is expendable. God, too, has plans. His Name must be sanctified and every Jew is a soldier in His army, fighting for the achievement of His goal. The loss of a single soldier is not insignificant to God, nor may it be to us. His kingdom has been diminished, as it were. So the heirs must fill the void by announcing to a congregation of fellow Jews that God's Name must be sanctified.

*The loss of a single soldier is not insignificant to God, nor may it be to us. His kingdom has been diminished.*

The Sages teach, 'Israel is beloved because they are called children of God' (*Avos* 3:14). A Jew is dead. His children have lost a parent. God has lost a son. His army has a void. Let us fill it. Let us comfort *both* fathers.

*A Jew is dead. His children have lost a parent. God has lost a son. His army has a void.*

> *May His great Name be exalted and sanctified! ... May His great Name be blessed forever and ever!*

# ﬠﬡﬨﬢﬣﬤﬥ קָדִישׁ וְקַדִישׁ שָׁלֵם ﬠﬡ

# ﬠﬡ Half and Full Kaddish

*Kaddish*, whose lofty significance has been discussed in the *Overview*, is an integral part of the daily communal prayers. Early commentators note that *Kaddish* should be heard at least seven times a day, but in practice it is recited much more frequently, especially when mourners are present during the services.

The basic *Kaddish* (stiches 1-8), is commonly known as חֲצִי קַדִּישׁ, *Half Kaddish*. The *chazzan* recites it to separate one section of a prayer unit from the next. During *Shacharis* [the morning prayer], for example, the *Half Kaddish* is said by the *chazzan* between the end of *Pesukei D'Zimrah* [the psalms from *Baruch She'amar* through *Yishtabach*] and *Borchu*, which begins the *Blessings of Shema*. The two portions are part of the *Shacharis* prayer order, but because they are separate and distinct units, they are separated by the *Half Kaddish*.

Upon conclusion of a complete prayer order, קַדִּישׁ שָׁלֵם, the *Full Kaddish* is recited by the *chazzan*. By definition, a 'complete' prayer order is one in which the *Shemoneh Esrei* has been recited. The *Full Kaddish* includes three additional stiches (9-11) which plead that God accept the just-concluded prayers and bless the congregation with peace and life. The subject of this *Kaddish*, therefore, is always *Shemoneh Esrei* even when such additional prayers as *Tachanun* and *Ashrei-U'Va L'Zion* are recited immediately after *Shemoneh Esrei*. The only exception to this rule is *Selichos*, which is followed by a *Full Kaddish*, although no *Shemoneh Esrei* has been said.

For the sake of easy cross-reference, we have taken the liberty of numbering the stiches of *Kaddish*. As the commentary will show, according to some of the interpretations the separation of stiches should be done otherwise; consequently our separation and numbering system should be taken as nothing more than a convenience.

וְעַתָּה יִגְדַּל נָא כֹּחַ אֲדֹנָי כַּאֲשֶׁר דִּבַּרְתָּ לֵאמֹר:
זְכֹר רַחֲמֶיךָ יהוה וַחֲסָדֶיךָ כִּי מֵעוֹלָם הֵמָּה:

<sub>אמן</sub>

# 1 יִתְגַּדַּל וְיִתְקַדַּשׁ שְׁמֵהּ רַבָּא.

### ◆§ Introductory Verses

There is a custom in some communities for the congregation to recite the following two verses — from *Numbers* 14:17 and *Psalms* 25:6 respectively — before the *chazzan* begins *Kaddish* (*Rama, O. Ch.* 56:1) because of their relevance to the themes of *Kaddish* (*Tur, Etz Yosef*). ARIzal, however, frowned on the custom and preferred that these verses not be said. Therefore, even those who retain the practice should not recite the verses at any time when it is forbidden to speak, such as between *Yishtabach* and *Borchu* (*Mishnah Berurah* 56 §11).

**וְעַתָּה יִגְדַּל נָא כֹּחַ אֲדֹנָי** — *And now may the power of my Lord be great.*

This verse, because it calls for the revelation of God's strength, expresses the theme of *Kaddish* as explained below (*Tur; Etz Yosef*).

Moses uttered these words as part of his prayer seeking to save Israel from destruction in punishment for its acceptance of the slanderous report of the spies and its refusal to have faith in God's promise of a successful conquest of *Eretz Yisrael* [*Numbers* 14:13-19]. Moses asked that God demonstrate His power by showing His willingness to be patient with the wicked as well as with the righteous (*Rashi*).

That God would suppress His Attribute of Justice despite the provocations of the sinful is a manifestation of Divine power (*Ramban; Sforno*).

[As we shall see below, *Kaddish* represents ultimate triumph of good over evil. This will not necessarily come about as a result of Israel's virtue; rather the Redemption can be the greatest proof that God suppresses judgment in order to bring benefit to the universe.]

**כַּאֲשֶׁר דִּבַּרְתָּ לֵאמֹר** — *As You declared, saying:*

When Moses was in heaven to receive the Torah, God informed him that Divine mercy extended even to the wicked. Moses now asked God to show this mercy to the sinful Jews (*Rashi*).

In the following verse in *Numbers* ibid., Moses went on to cite the specific attributes needed to save Israel at this particular juncture (*Ramban*).

**זְכֹר רַחֲמֶיךָ ה' וַחֲסָדֶיךָ** — *Remember Your mercies, HASHEM, and Your kindnesses.*

God's mercy upon a human being begins from the very moment of conception. It continues through birth and development to maturity. The Psalmist asks God to remember and continue this boundless mercy (*Radak*).

**כִּי מֵעוֹלָם הֵמָּה** — *For they are from the beginning of the world.*

In the universal sense, God's mercy upon mankind began on the day Adam was created. Although Adam was warned that he would die on the day he ate from the tree (*Genesis* 2:17), God gave him nearly a thousand years of life. May such a display of mercy be remembered and extended to all sinners (*Rashi*).

[Thus, this verse recalls the attribute of mercy which, we pray in *Kaddish*, will bring the final Redemption and sanctification of God's Name.]

### ◆§ The Kaddish

**1. יִתְגַּדַּל וְיִתְקַדַּשׁ** — *May ... be exalted and sanctified.*

*Kaddish* is a plea for the ultimate sanctification of God's Name through the redemption of Israel, and it expresses the concept that Israel's national purpose is to

*And now, may the power of my Lord be great*
*as You declared, saying:*
*Remember Your mercies, HASHEM, and your kindnesses,*
*for they are from the beginning of the world.*

## ¹ M ay His great Name be exalted and sanctified

Congregation responds: *Amen.*

achieve recognition of God's sovereignty everywhere on earth. This is a communal responsibility, for the Divine Presence rests upon a community; the greater the number, the more intense the Presence. For this reason, *Kaddish*, like other communal דְּבָרִים שֶׁבִּקְדֻשָׁה, *expressions of sanctification*, may be recited only in the presence of a *minyan* [a quorum of at least ten males above thirteen, the age of *bar mitzvah*], the smallest number of people which may be considered to represent the community. Individuals, too, are required by the Torah to sanctify God's Name, but only the nation can achieve this goal to its ultimate degree *(R' Hirsch; R' Munk).*

R' Yehudah ben Yakar finds support for the interpretation that God's Name will be sanctified only by virtue of the joint efforts of the Jewish People in the *Mechilta (Exodus* 15:1): כְּשֶׁיִּשְׂרָאֵל עוֹשִׂין רְצוֹנוֹ שֶׁל מָקוֹם אָז מִתְגַּדֵּל שְׁמוֹ שֶׁל הקב"ה *When Israel does the will of the Omnipresent, then the Name of the Holy One, Blessed be He, is exalted.*

The opening phrase is based on God's declaration וְהִתְגַּדִּלְתִּי וְהִתְקַדִּשְׁתִּי, *And I will be exalted and sanctified (Ezekiel* 38:23). The context of this phrase in *Ezekiel* reveals its intended meaning in *Kaddish*. The prophet has told of the future cataclysmic war of Gog and Ma-

gog, when all the nations on earth will unite in a struggle against God's Chosen People. The result will be the total defeat of the nations and the universal acknowledgment of God's infinite greatness and might. The implication of this expression of praise is not that God will *become* greater — for He is infinite and unchanging — but that only then when His greatness will finally be recognized universally, will the ultimate קִדּוּשׁ הַשֵּׁם, *Sanctification of the Name*, take place.

The commentators clearly link this development with the end of Israel's current Edomite Exile, for in addition to the above prophecy of Ezekiel, they relate this prayer to two other prophecies which refer to Israel's ultimate emergence from Edom's dominion and its establishment of God's uncontested kingdom. Those prophecies are: וְעָלוּ מוֹשִׁעִים בְּהַר צִיּוֹן לִשְׁפֹּט אֶת הַר עֵשָׂו וְהָיְתָה לַה' הַמְּלוּכָה, *Then saviors* [Messiah and Jewish judges *(Ibn Ezra and Radak)*] *will go up to Mount Zion to judge Esau, and the kingdom shall be HASHEM's (Obadiah* 1:21); וְהָיָה ה' לְמֶלֶךְ עַל כָּל הָאָרֶץ בַּיּוֹם הַהוּא יִהְיֶה ה' אֶחָד וּשְׁמוֹ אֶחָד, *HASHEM will be King over all the world — on that day HASHEM will be One and His Name will be One (Zechariah* 14:9) *(R' Yehudah ben Yakar, Abudraham, Shibbolei HaLeket).*

יִתְגַּדֵּל — *May ... be exalted.*

[The root of the word is גדל, *great*, and it is commonly translated as *be magnified*, which suggests that God will eventually become greater than He is at present. Since this is clearly erroneous — and even blasphemous, for it is a principle of Jewish faith that God is perfect, and therefore unchanging — we have translated יִתְגַּדֵּל as *... be exalted.* The sense of the word is that He will someday be acknowledged as great by *all mankind* (see below).]

[However, according to one interpretation cited below, the rendering *magnified* is justified.]

A particular connotation is inherent in the use of the root גדל, which refers to 'greatness.' Our prayer is that God be exalted through the universal acknowledgment of His גְּדֻלָה, *greatness. Maharal* (*Gevuras Hashem* ch. 69) describes this attribute as evidenced by the fact that He alone created the entire universe with all the conditions, potential, and nations needed for it to achieve the purpose ordained by Him.

וְיִתְקַדַּשׁ — *And ... [be] sanctified.*[1]

Here too, we pray *not* that God *become* holy, for He is the unchanging zenith of holiness. Rather we pray that His holiness be acknowledged by all mankind, a circumstance which will come to pass only with the final Redemption.

*Dover Shalom* comments that יִתְגַּדֵּל, *be exalted*, refers to the recognition of God's greatness as exemplified by His deeds, while

וְיִתְקַדַּשׁ, *be sanctified*, refers to a recognition of the sanctity of His Essence, entirely apart from whether or how He manifests this in ways obvious enough for us to perceive.

## ◈§ Vocalization of יִתְגַּדֵּל וְיִתְקַדַּשׁ.

There are two widespread customs concerning the vocalization of the first two words of *Kaddish*, both customs based on views of halachic and grammatical authorities. *Mishnah Berurah* [56:2] rules that the words should be read יִתְגַּדֵּל וְיִתְקַדֵּשׁ [*Yisgadeil v'yiskadeish.*] This follows the ruling of *Pri Megadim* and the *Vilna Gaon* in *Maaseh Rav* [55]. *Avodas Yisrael, Siddur Tehillas Hashem,* and *Tzelusa d'Avraham* rule that the proper pronunciation is יִתְגַּדַּל וְיִתְקַדַּשׁ [*Yisgadal v'yiskadash*].

The controversy revolves around the language of the *Kaddish*. The proper Hebrew form would be יִתְגַּדֵּל, while the Aramaic form would be יִתְגַּדַּל. *Mishnah Berurah* notes that the two opening words are clearly Hebrew because the Aramaic equivalent would be יִתְרַבֵּי וְיִתְקַדַּשׁ — therefore the vocalization must be in the Hebrew form, יִתְגַּדֵּל. Those who subscribe to the Aramaic vocalization imply that the Hebrew root גדל was retained because it alludes to the phrase in *Ezekiel* 38:23 upon which the *Kaddish* is based, as explained above, but since the rest of *Kaddish* was rendered into Aramaic, the Aramaic *vocalization* was adapted for the first two words, as well. *Emek Brachah* ex-

---

1. [While the term קדש generally connotes holiness, it *literally* refers to the condition of *separation* or being *cut off*. God is 'separate' because He is infinitely above all else in creation, whether physical or spiritual. In a borrowed sense, a human being who sanctifies himself by withdrawing even from permissible physical pleasure and temptation in order to devote himself to the service of God, is called *holy*; he too has separated himself from the mass of humanity.

Even those who have cut themselves off from others by falling drastically *below* the norm of decent behavior, however, may be described by a form of this term. Thus, in *Deuteronomy* 23:18, male and female harlots are referred to respectively as קָדֵשׁ and קְדֵשָׁה. (See *Rashi* and *Ramban* to *Lev.* 19:2; *Ramban* to *Deut.* 23:18).

The intent of the *Kaddish* prayer is that God come to be acknowledged and acclaimed as *sanctified* in the sense that He is elevated above all that exists.]

plains further that these two Hebrew words were so familiar even to unlearned, Aramaic-speaking people, that there was no necessity to translate them into Aramaic.

### שְׁמֵהּ רַבָּא — His great Name.

The translation follows the consensus of most commentators although, as we shall see below, there is a different interpretation of this phrase. This phrase, which begins the Aramaic text of the Kaddish, is translated in the Talmud as שְׁמוֹ הַגָּדוֹל, His great Name (Berachos 3a). That His 'Name,' is the object of praise rather than God Himself is frequently found in Scripture. In depicting the eventual universal recognition of God's Omnipotence, the prophets refer to the time when יִהְיֶה ... שְׁמוֹ אֶחָד, His 'Name' will be One [Zechariah 14:9]. Similarly Daniel [2:20] prayed: לֶהֱוֵא שְׁמֵהּ דִּי אֱלָהָא מְבָרַךְ, let the Name of God be blessed.

Our spelling of the word שְׁמֵהּ without a yud [rather than שְׁמֵיהּ] is in accordance with the above interpretation. For, as Mor U'Ketziah [ch. 56] notes, in the Aramaic Books of Ezra and Daniel it is always spelled שְׁמֵהּ. R' Yaakov Emden (gloss to Berachos 3a) explains that the Talmudic spelling includes a yud only for the convenience of the reader; since the Talmudic text is unvocalized, the reader might mistakenly read the word שְׁמֵהּ if the yud were omitted. Such added letters to facilitate proper pronunciation are common in Talmudic spelling.

Several early commentators, such as Machzor Vitry [cited by Tosafos, Berachos 3a s.v. וְעוֹנִין: Abudra-

ham; and Tur, Orach Chaim 56], however, have a much different interpretation of the phrase. According to them, the word שְׁמֵיהּ, spelled with a yud, is a contraction of the two words שֵׁם יָהּ, Name of God. In their view, the opening prayer of the Kaddish is based on the following Midrash: אֵין שְׁמוֹ שָׁלֵם וְאֵין כִּסְאוֹ שָׁלֵם עַד שֶׁיִּמָּחֶה שְׁמוֹ שֶׁל עֲמָלֵק, [God's] Name cannot be whole nor can His throne be whole until the name of Amalek is erased (Tanchuma, Vayeitzei, cited by Rashi to Exodus 17:16).

The sense of the Midrash is that God's glory, as represented by the Name יָהּ, is diminished by the continued existence of the forces of evil. Only at the End of Days when the enemies of God and Israel are finally and totally defeated, will God's Name emerge in its full glory.

According to this interpretation, the opening of the Kaddish would be rendered: May the great Name 'Yah' become enlarged [i.e. may the deficient Name יָהּ become expanded to the full expression of God's glory as represented by the Four-Letter Name] and sanctified.[1]

### אָמֵן — Amen.

[At this point, the congregation responds אָמֵן, Amen (Rambam, Seder Tefillos; Aruch HaShulchan 56:6). This is the only place in the Kaddish where the congregation responds Amen without having

---

1. R' Yehudah ben Yakar, too, interprets שְׁמֵיהּ as a contraction of שֵׁם יָהּ, Name of God, however he adduces a different reason for the use of that particular Name. The Talmud [Menachos 29b] teaches that God created heaven by uttering the letter ה, and the earth by uttering the letter י, and that these two facets of creation are implicit in the Name יָהּ, which is formed by those two letters. In praying for the exaltation and sanctification of God's Name, we ask that He be universally acknowledged as the Creator of all, and we therefore refer to Him by the Name that identifies Him as Creator of heaven and earth.

This formula parallels that of עַל הַכֹּל [Al HaKol], Above Everything, the prayer recited on the Sabbath morning while the Torah Scroll is carried from the Ark to the bimah [reading table]. Many commentators note the strong parallelism between Kaddish and Al HaKol. There, too, we pray that God be praised throughout the universe: in This World and in the World to Come.

בְּעָלְמָא דִּי בְרָא כִרְעוּתֵהּ. וְיַמְלִיךְ 2
מַלְכוּתֵהּ. 3 (וְיַצְמַח פֻּרְקָנֵהּ וִיקָרֵב מְשִׁיחֵהּ.
(אָמֵן)

been explicitly requested to do so by the declaration, וְאִמְרוּ אָמֵן, *Now respond, Amen.* These first four words of the *Kaddish* contain the essential message of the prayer — that God's Name be sanctified to the ultimate degree. It is to this prayer of the leader that the later response יְהֵא שְׁמֵהּ רַבָּא, *may His Great Name ... is* directed (see below). As the *comm.* below will make clear, the phrases that intervene between the first expression of the prayer and that major response are parenthetical insertions that further clarify — but do not add to — the message of the opening phrase. Therefore, it would be improper not to respond *Amen* to this expression of longing for the fulfillment of creation's purpose. The full response of *Yehei Shmei Rabbah* to which the Sages attach such cosmic implications (see *Overview* and *comm.* below) is recited later after the intervening phrases clarify in more detail the implications of the key prayer with which the *Kaddish* begins.]

The word אָמֵן stands for אֵל מֶלֶךְ נֶאֱמָן, God, *the trustworthy King* (*Shabbos* 119b), and is derived from the same root as אֱמוּנָה, *faithfulness* (*Tur, Orach Chaim* 124). As such, it is a declaration that the listener subscribes with unquestioning faith and belief to what has just been pronounced by the reader. This declaration can have two connotations, depending on the context. If it follows a *blessing* or other statement in praise of God, the responsive *Amen* signifies that the listener agrees with the statement. If it follows a *prayer*, whether stated as a

blessing or in another form, the *Amen* contains a further connotation: not only does the listener agree that God alone has the power to answer prayer, but he, the listener, joins the reader in praying that the desired result will be granted. In *Kaddish*, the *Amen* expresses both an acknowledgment that His Name will indeed be exalted and sanctified in the time to come, and that we pray for this to happen (*Mishnah Berurah* 124 §25).

**2. בְּעָלְמָא דִּי בְרָא כִרְעוּתֵהּ** — *In the world He created according to His will.*

God created the concept of this perfect world before He created the universe [i.e., His wisdom dictated that such a state of perfection must exist *eventually*, because creation could not achieve its purpose unless such a state would eventually come into existence] *(Ran).*

*R' Yehudah ben Yakar* interprets the phrase as a reference to the world of the *future.* It is described here in the *past* tense, however, because God created the universe with the wish that mankind would fulfill its mission on earth so that all evil would be defeated and the world would become perfect. Since *Kaddish* is a prayer for an exaltation of God's Name that is possible only when all peoples recognize His greatness [see above], we now pray for the kind of world which He desired — where His Name will be exalted and sanctified. This form of existence — a world of goodness, free from evil — is known as גַּן עֵדֶן, literally *Garden of Eden,* or

**2** *in the world He created according to His will;*
*And may He establish His Kingship*
**3** *(and cause His salvation to sprout and bring near*
*His Messiah —*     Congregation responds: *Amen.)*

עוֹלָם הַבָּא, *the World to Come.*

*Abudraham* describes the universe as it *now* exists as the world created according to God's will. We find in *Bereishis Rabbah* 8:4 that God consulted the angels before creating man. [There (8:7) it is further stated that He consulted the souls of the righteous before creating the universe.] However, when heaven and earth were created on the first day, the angels [and the souls] were not yet in existence. Only God's will was involved in the original creation.[1]

*Dover Shalom* refers this phrase to the Midrashic comment that God created other worlds and rejected them before He created the one in which we live [*Bereishis Rabbah* 3:7]; therefore our universe is described as the one that conforms to His will.

*Vilna Gaon* interprets as follows: בְּעָלְמָא דִי בְרָא, *in the world which He created*, is a parenthetical phrase describing the setting in which we pray for the exaltation of God's Name; while כִּרְעוּתֵהּ, *according to His will*, reverts to the beginning of *Kaddish*. Thus *Vilna Gaon* renders:

יִתְגַּדֵּל וְיִתְקַדֵּשׁ שְׁמֵהּ רַבָּא בְּעָלְמָא דִי בְרָא, *May His Great Name be exalted and sanctified — in the world which He created*; כִּרְעוּתֵהּ, [And may this exaltation take place] *according to His will*. Thus, we pray for fulfillment of God's wish that His Name be sanctified on earth. Support for this interpretation is found in עַל הַכֹּל, the prayer said on the Sabbath while the Torah is taken in the reading table. As noted above, that prayer and *Kaddish* closely parallel one another. There, too, hope is expressed that God's Name be exalted and sanctified כִּרְצוֹנוֹ, *according to His will.*

וְיַמְלִיךְ מַלְכוּתֵהּ — *And may He establish His Kingship.*

This plea makes explicit what had been suggested earlier: that we pray for God to be acknowledged by all as the sovereign ruler of everything that exists (*Abudraham*).

**3.** וְיַצְמַח פֻּרְקָנֵהּ וִיקָרֵב מְשִׁיחֵהּ — *And cause His salvation to sprout and bring near His Messiah.*

[These two phrases are found in various early versions of *Kaddish*,

1. *Gesher HaChaim* comments that the plan of the universe often seems incomprehensible to man, filled as it is with so many apparent contradictions. Man, especially, with his capacity for infinite good and infinite evil, seems to be a study in contrasts. People may well think that they would have made the universe differently — and better. But despite the limitations of human understanding, God made creation exactly as *He* wished, and according to the dictates of His unfathomable wisdom. In a deeper sense, this is an acknowledgment that no part of creation, from the minutest organism to the mightiest star, is without purpose in God's master plan.

*Gesher HaChaim* notes further that this declaration has particular relevance to the role of *Kaddish* as a mourner's prayer. Despite his sense of personal loss and tragedy, the mourner acknowledges that all is according to God's will. Nothing, not even his loss, happens at random or without reason.

[31]     *Kaddish*

among them *Rambam* and *Abudraham*. They continue the prayer for God's kingship by adding pleas for the emergence of His salvation and Messiah. These phrases generally are included in the *Kaddish* of *Nusach Sfard*, but omitted in *Nusach Ashkenaz*. *Aruch HaShulchan* explains the reason for their omission: both salvation and Messiah are essential components of God's above mentioned kingdom, therefore it is unnecessary to mention them specifically.]

וְיַצְמַח פֻּרְקָנֵהּ — *And cause His salvation to sprout.*

*Iyun Tefillah* cites *Midrash Shocher Tov* [Psalms 18:51] that the Redemption will come to Israel in stages, like a gradually sprouting plant, because the shock of a sudden and complete Redemption would be more than the people could bear.

The phrase is an Aramaic translation of מַצְמִיחַ יְשׁוּעָה, found near the end of the second blessing of *Shemoneh Esrei*. *Abudraham* derives it from יַצְמִיחַ צְדָקָה וּתְהִלָּה נֶגֶד כָּל הַגּוֹיִם, [Just as the earth yields vegetation, God] *will cause righteousness and praise to sprout* [for Israel] *in the face of the nations* (Isaiah 61:11). *Emek Brachah* derives it from the following verse in *Ezekiel* 29:21: בַּיּוֹם הַהוּא אַצְמִיחַ קֶרֶן לְבֵית יִשְׂרָאֵל, *on that day I will cause the pride of Israel to sprout.*

וְקָרֵב מְשִׁיחֵהּ — *And bring near His Messiah.*

This is the logical conclusion of the prayer for salvation, for there can be no redemption, in fulfillment of the Scriptural prophecies, without the advent of Messiah, the scion of David (*Emek Brachah*).

*Abudraham* adds the word קֵץ — וְקָרֵב קֵץ מְשִׁיחֶה, *and bring near the appointed time* [lit. *End*] *of his Messiah*, i.e., the time beyond which

there can be no further delay of the *Messiah's* coming. The implication is that even if we do not merit redemption at this moment, may God decree that the deadline for Messiah's coming is upon us.

**4.** בְּחַיֵּיכוֹן וּבְיוֹמֵיכוֹן — *During your lifetime and during your days.*

This phrase addresses itself to those who are present during the recitation of *Kaddish*. The person reciting the prayer is not content to pray only that God's glory be revealed and that *he* be witness to that momentous event — he adds the prayer that all his companions be privileged to live and participate in the great happening (*Siddur Bais Yaakov*).

However, although the phrase is in the plural, it is in *second* person, not first: The reader does not say בְּחַיָּנָא וּבְיוֹמָנָא, *in our lifetime and in our days,* because the structure of *Kaddish* is that of a leader urging his community to respond to and associate itself with his prayer for Sanctification of the Name. Thus, the sections of *Kaddish* are concluded with וְאִמְרוּ אָמֵן, *now* [you listeners] *respond Amen* (*Gesher HaChaim*).

*Aruch HaShulchan* adds that this is also a prayer that the final Redemption take place soon — while we are still alive to see it.

When the Redemption is at hand, only a relatively small number of people will deserve to be part of it, as Jeremiah said, אֶחָד מֵעִיר וּשְׁנַיִם מִמִּשְׁפָּחָה, *one from a city and two from a family* (Jeremiah 3:14). Therefore, we pray that every one of our compatriots will be among those who live to see and take part in the Redemption (*Abudraham*).

*R' Munk* comments that this section of *Kaddish* expresses the conviction

<sup>4</sup> *during your lifetime and during your days*
*and during the lifetime of the entire*
*Family of Israel,*
<sup>5</sup> *swiftly and soon.*

*Now respond: Amen.*

Congregation responds: *Amen.*

---

that not only will the goal of Sanctification of the Name ultimately be realized, but also the faith that every Jewish generation and individual has a share in achieving the Sanctification.

וּבְחַיֵּי דְכָל בֵּית יִשְׂרָאֵל — *And during the lifetime of the entire Family* [lit. *house*] *of Israel.*

The obvious connotation of the phrase is that we extend our prayer from those in our immediate company to the entire nation.

*Bais Yaakov* interprets this as a special prayer for the leaders of Israel. The Sages have taught that with the arrival of the destined time of a new leader, the old one must pass from the scene; he can neither delay, interfere, nor compete with the emergence of the new leader. This being so, we pray that the present authorities of Israel be permitted to enjoy the coming of the Messianic king.

דְכָל ... — *Of the entire ...*

It is a consistent rule of Scriptural and Mishnaic interpretation that the word כָּל, *entire* or *all*, is meant to imply a רִבּוּי, an *addition* to whatever is explicitly enumerated. The word כָּל in our context implies that the reader includes *himself* too in the House of Israel; were he to say only וּבְחַיֵּי דְבֵית יִשְׂרָאֵל, *and in the lifetime of the Family of Israel,* one might infer that he means all Jews with the exception of himself. For this reason, the formula כָּל בֵּית

יִשְׂרָאֵל is used consistently during public prayers, as it is here and later in *Kaddish (Iyun Tefillah* to *Shemoneh Esrei).*

**5.** בַּעֲגָלָא וּבִזְמַן קָרִיב — *Swiftly and soon* [lit. *and in a near time*].

We pray that God's sovereignty be established without delay. Although the two terms are similar, they express different ideas. The Sages teach *(Sanhedrin 97ff)* that the epoch of the Messiah may be preceded by a long, drawn-out period of agony known as חֶבְלֵי מָשִׁיחַ, *the birth pains of Messiah.* Some *Tannaim* went so far as to declare that while they prayed for Messiah's coming, they hoped they would not be alive to endure the upheavals of the period. Therefore, בַּעֲגָלָא, *swiftly,* is a prayer that God mercifully cut short the period of suffering — may the trauma, if it must come, be brief and end *swiftly.* Nevertheless, we do not wish to defer Messiah's emergence; to the contrary, we pray that he come בִּזְמַן קָרִיב, as *soon* as possible *(Aruch HaShulchan).*

וְאִמְרוּ אָמֵן — *Now respond, Amen.*

The congregation responds *Amen* to signify its concurrence with the prayer just concluded [see above s.v. אָמֵן] and goes on to amplify its statement by devoutly and clearly declaring its hope that God's Name will be blessed forever *(Aruch HaShulchan).*

## ◄§ Yehei Shmei Rabbah

**6.** יְהֵא שְׁמֵהּ רַבָּא — *May His Great Name ...*

[The *Talmud* stresses in several places that *Yehei Shmei Rabbah* has an enormous cosmic effect. Indeed, the *halachah* states that an opportunity to hear *Kaddish* and respond *Yehei Shmei Rabbah* takes precedence over an opportunity to respond to any other prayer, even *Kedushah* and *Borchu* (*Orach Chaim* 56:1, *Mishnah Berurah* §6). This aspect of *Yehei Shmei Rabbah* is discusssed in the *Overview*.]

The *Talmud* (*Shabbos* 119b) teaches that one must recite *Yehei Shmai Rabbah* בְּכָל כֹּחוֹ, *with all his 'strength'*. *Rashi* and *Tosafos* there interpret this to mean בְּכָל כַּוָּנָתוֹ, *with all his concentration*. *R' Yonah* comments that the essential requirement is for *concentration*, but since people tend to pray with more feeling when they pray *loudly*, it is advisable to raise one's voice when saying *Yehei Shmei Rabbah*. Nevertheless, one should not say it so loudly that he will invite ridicule.

However, *Tosafos* (*Shabbos* 119b) cites the *Pesikta*, and *Bais Yosef* (*O. Ch.* 56) cites the *Zohar* that a loud response is important in its own right, and not as a device to achieve maximum concentration. Even so, *Mishnah Berurah* (56 §6) rules that *R' Yonah's* admonition not to respond with excessive loudness applies even according to *Pesikta* and *Zohar*.

Although citing the ruling that one should not shout excessively, *Gesher HaChaim* infers that, unlike the general principle that a congregant's response should never be louder than the reader's (*Orach Chaim* 124:12), this rule does not apply to *Yehei Shmei Rabbah*, for which a loud response is meritorious. However, *Kaf HaChaim* (*O. Ch.* 55:15) disagrees.

*Maharal* (*Nesiv HaTefillah* 12) gives a third interpretation of בְּכָל כֹּחוֹ, *with all his strength*: *Yehei Shmei Rabbah* must be enunciated clearly in order to achieve the cosmic results of which it is capable. [See *Overview*.]

מְבָרַךְ — *Be blessed.*

[The expression 'blessing' implies that the blesser confers some benefit on the one he blesses. Clearly, God can bless people, even human beings can bless one another; but how can a person presume to bless God, as though it were in his power to give God something?]

— *Sefer HaChinuch* (*mitzvah* 430) explains that the expression 'blessing' as applied to God does *not* mean that we presume to give Him something. Rather it is an acknowledgment that He *is* blessed, in the sense that He is perfect and complete. [According to this, הַקָּדוֹשׁ בָּרוּךְ הוּא should be rendered. *The Holy One, Blessed 'is' He*, and not *Blessed 'be' He*.] In *Kaddish*, therefore, we pray that the acknowledgment become universal.

— *Rashba* (*Teshuvos* 5:51) and *R' Bachya* (*Kad HaKemach*) derive the word בְּרָכָה, *blessing*, from בְּרֵכָה, *a spring*. Just as a spring flows constantly with fresh supplies of water, so God is the Source of inexhaustible blessing. By 'blessing' Him, we express the realization that He created the universe as a vehicle to enable Him to do good to others. Our blessings express the implied prayer that we be deserving of

## 6 May His great Name be blessed forever and ever.

God's abundant mercy. In *Kaddish*, we pray for the final Redemption, when mankind will be elevated to the spiritual level of Adam before his sin. That infinitely heightened state of spiritual attainment will enable us to benefit from God's goodness to the degree He intended when He created the universe.

— *R' Hirsch* interprets the declaration 'Blessed are You' as a pledge to fulfill God's will. Thus, given the changed world order which will come into existence after the Redemption, we now declare that that ·era will be one of total dedication to Him.

ﻉ§ **Alternate rendering.**

As noted above, *Machzor Vitry*, as well as other authoritative commentators, hold that the word שְׁמֵיהּ [*shmei*] is a contraction of the words שֵׁם יָהּ, *Name of God*. According to this rendering, *Yehei Shmei Rabbah* ... consists of two parts:

(a) יְהֵא שְׁמֵיהּ רַבָּא, *May the Name of God become enlarged*, i.e., the glory of God, as signified by His Name, is diminished by the ascendancy of the forces of evil. May good triumph over evil so that His abbreviated Name can become expanded to the Four-Letter Name that symbolizes His full majesty.

(b) Now we go on to pray ... וּמְבָרַךְ לְעָלַם, *And may it [the Name of God] be blessed forever ... (Tur O.Ch. 56).*

The fact that the *Talmud* constantly cites the word מְבָרַך, *be blessed*, without the prefix ו, and, is cited by *Tosafos (Berachos* 3a s.v. וְעוֹנִין) as a refutation of *Machzor Vitry's* rendering.

לְעָלַם וּלְעָלְמֵי עָלְמַיָּא — *Forever and ever* [lit., *for eternity and for eternity of eternities*].

May the future ascendancy of God be eternal. Unlike the glorious periods of the First and Second Temples which ended in destruction and exile, the epoch of the Third Temple will endure forever *(Aruch HaShulchan).* [1]

1. *Nefesh HaChaim* (1:2) interprets differently based on the other familiar translation of עוֹלָם [or, in Aramaic, עָלַם], *world*. The literal translation of the expression is לְעָלַם, *to the world* [singular], וּלְעָלְמֵי, *and to the worlds* [plural], עָלְמַיָּא, *of the world* [again singular.] The combination of terms yields a total of *four worlds.* Indeed, the Kabbalah teaches that there are four worlds which are intermediary stages of existence between God and man. It is axiomatic that man can have no contact with or comprehension of the Divine level of holiness. The descent from a higher 'world' to a lower 'world' may be likened to the attempt to simplify a concept from the terms of advanced scholarship to those of graduate school, to secondary, elementary, and primary levels. The four 'worlds' are:

(1) אֲצִילוּת, *Emanation,* the one closest to God Himself, a stage of existence beyond all human comprehension. This is the world of the expression לְעָלַם in *Kaddish.*

(2) בְּרִיאָה, *Creation,* a definite state of existence, although one that is still far beyond human intelligence.

(3) יְצִירָה, *Formation,* in which the spirituality of the earlier worlds becomes shaped into a closer approximation of our everyday existence.

(4) עֲשִׂיָּה, *Deed,* the world of action, cause and effect, and natural law in which we live.

The first, and highest, of these four worlds is referred to with the singular term לְעָלַם, *to the world.* The second and third worlds are represented by the plural expression וּלְעָלְמֵי, *and to the worlds.* These two transitory worlds, which are the bridge between the first stage of Creation and our own lives, are lumped into a single plural term in *Kaddish.* The fourth and final world, our world, is the one. mentioned last in our phrase.

The four worlds of creation are paralleled by levels of holiness in man's *personal* spiritual constellation. Thus, the connotation of this pivotal declaration in *Kaddish* is that we pray for God's greatness to be manifested in every stage of universal history and existence and also in every stage of man's own life and performance.

The phrase is based on *Daniel 7:18 (R' Yehudah ben Yakar, Abudraham)* or *Daniel 2:20 (Iyun Tefillah; Avodas Yisrael)*. It is also *Onkelos'* rendition of לְעוֹלָם וָעֶד, *forever and ever (Exodus 15:18)*.

*Ibn Ezra, Radak* and *R' Hirsch* to *Psalms 41:4* render עוֹלָם as a reference to time: *from times past throughout the future*. *R' Hirsch (Genesis 21:33)* relates עוֹלָם, eternal time to הֶעְלֵם, hiddenness. The significance of all time is hidden from us. Our knowledge of the past is indefinite, and our most confident predictions of the future are frequently disappointed. Furthermore, even our perception of the present is far from perfect, for we cannot be certain what gave birth to it and where it will lead. Of one thing we can be sure — all of time is a chain leading up to the ultimate goal ordained by God. Only upon its conclusion will people be able to look back and comprehend how each event was a necessary part of the sequence. When the Redemption comes, we will understand how each element in passing time was a necessary preamble to the fulfillment of God's will.

Similarly, many commentators explain that the very universe is given a name, עוֹלָם, that connotes hiddenness, because the natural, physical laws under which the universe functions tend to obscure the power — even the existence — of God. The purpose of presenting man with a world in which Godliness can be overlooked is to allow him to exercise his free choice to find the truth from within the concealment. Thus, our prayer is that God's Name come to be blessed even on earth where perception of His greatness has been so clouded.

◆§ **Numerical significance of Yehei Shmei Rabbah.**

The stich *Yehei Shmei Rabbah* contains seven words and twenty-eight letters. The commentators cite various esoteric allusions intended by these numbers.

— *Bais Yosef* cites *Mahari Aboav* that the first verse of the Torah [*Genesis 1:1*] and the verse introducing the Ten Commandments [*Exodus 20:1*] each contain seven words and twenty-eight letters. The Sages formulated *Yehei Shmei Rabbah* to recall those two verses. [The first verse of *Genesis* introduces physical existence while *Exodus 20:1* introduces the expression of God's will, which is the purpose of Creation and, as such, the life-giving 'soul' of physical existence. By praying for the time when God's Name will be universally exalted, we allude to the conviction that history is leading to the time when creation and its purpose become united.]

— The twenty-eight letters allude to the *Talmud's* requirement that we are to recite *Yehei Shmei Rabbah* with all our כֹּחַ, *strength* (see above), since the word כֹּחַ has the numerical value of twenty-eight (*Bais Yosef, Avodas Yisrael*).

— The seven words allude to the שִׁבְעָה רְקִיעִים, *seven heavens* (*Avodas Yisrael*).

[The *Vilna Gaon (Hilchos Rosh Chodesh)* explains that the 'seven heavens' are seven levels of holiness separating man from God. Thus, it may be that the significance of this allusion is to suggest our hope that God's greatness be recognized throughout the layers separating Him from us, so that His holiness will be apparent even on earth.]

— The number twenty-eight has the further connotation of alluding to the verse כֹּחַ מַעֲשָׂיו הִגִּיד לְעַמּוֹ לָתֵת לָהֶם נַחֲלַת גּוֹיִם, *The power of His deeds He displayed to His nation by giving them the heritage of the peoples (Psalms 111:6)*. [*Rashi* explains that God demonstrates His mastery of the world by assigning land to whomever He wishes, as He did when He took *Eretz Yisrael* from the Canaanites and gave it to Israel. Or, as *Midrash Tanchuma* comments, God revealed Himself in the Torah as the Creator of the universe in order to justify Israel's right to *Eretz Yisrael*; since God created the world, it is His to distribute as He sees fit.] For this reason, too, there are exactly twenty-eight words from *Yehei* until the end of the 'Half' *Kaddish*. [The words וְאִמְרוּ אָמֵן, *now respond Amen*, are not included in the total since they are not part of *Kaddish*] (*Bais Yosef*).

— In *Ecclesiastes* 3:2-8, King Solomon lists twenty-eight 'times' which run the gamut of human experience: *A time to be born and a time to die; a time to plant and a time to uproot* ... The underlying theme is that in every stage of life and every form of existence, man must search for the way to utilize it to serve God. The twenty-eight letters in *Yehei Shmei Rabbah* and the similar number of words in this section of *Kaddish* allude to that concept.

[The requirement that *Yehei Shmei Rabbah* must contain twenty-eight letters is the cause of difficulty regarding the spelling of some of the words. As we have seen above, some commentators spell שְׁמֵיהּ with a *yud* because it is a contraction of the two words שֵׁם יָהּ, *the Name of God*. According to some others, it should be spelled with a *yud* even if it is the Aramaic form of שְׁמוֹ, *His Name*. If so, there are twenty-*nine* letters in this formula. Some commentators resolve the difficulty by omitting a letter from וּלְעָלְמֵי, some omit the prefix *vav*, while others omit the suffix *yud*. According to *Machzor Vitry* cited above that in addition to the *yud* of שְׁמֵיהּ, there is a *vav* as prefix in וּמְבָרַךְ, the problem is aggravated further. *Bais Yosef* insists that we have no right to tamper with a traditional formula for the sake of a numerical allusion. However, he concludes, according to the spelling שְׁמֵהּ, without a *yud*, there is no problem. This is an additional reason why we have adopted the spelling שְׁמֵהּ in our text.]

### ◆§ Is Amen part of the Yehei Shmei Rabbah?

The universal custom is to respond, '*Amen — Yehei Shmei Rabbah ...*' Simply understood, the *Amen* would seem to express an affirmation of the

*chazzan's* earlier declaration, while *Yehei Shmei Rabbah* is a new and separate response on the part of the congregation. However, as will be noted below, there are indications that the two responses are one. This question can have *halachic* implications. The *halachah* is that *Yehei Shmei Rabbah* should be said even during *Krias Shema* which may not be interrupted for an ordinary *Amen*. Does the *Amen* preceding *Yehei Shmei Rabbah* share this degree of importance? — It does if it is part of the response. Further, as we have seen above, there is significance in the number of words and letters of *Yehei Shmei Rabbah*. Does *Amen* upset these numerical allusions?

In discussing the congregational response during *Kaddish*, the *Talmud* (*Shabbos* 119b) speaks of the community answering *Amen Yehei Shmei Rabbah*. Elsewhere, however, (*Berachos* 3a; *Succah* 9a; *Sotah* 49a) *Amen* is *not* mentioned. Nevertheless, *Rambam, Tur, Bais Yosef* and *Aruch HaShulchan* include *Amen* as part of the response; while the text of *Shulchan Aruch* (*O. Ch.* 56) appears not to include it.

*Mor U'Ketziah* maintains that *Amen* must be attached to *Yehei Shmei Rabbah* [since both are in affirmation of and in response to what has been said by the reader (*Emek Brachah*)], especially since the merit of *Amen* in acknowledgment of the reader's words is even greater than that of the personal statement *Yehei Shmei Rabbah* [see *Overview*].

Nevertheless although the two responses are related, they still remain distinct, since *Amen* is purely an acknowledgment of the reader's words while *Yehei Shmei Rabbah* is a declaration of the congregant (*Gesher HaChaim*). [This combination of relationship and distinction is further indicated by the ruling of *Mishnah Berurah* 56 §9.]

A further indication that *Amen* must be regarded as separate is found in the significance of the seven words and twenty-eight letters discussed above. If *Amen* were considered an integral part of *Yehei Shmei Rabbah* there would be *eight* words and *thirty-one* letters.

[However, see *Overview*, where Maharal's interpretation of *Amen* as an eighth word is discussed.]

**⌑§ Where does the Yehei Shmei Rabbah response end?**

There are three opinions, each of which is supported by major early commentators.

(a) *Abudraham, R' Saadiah, Rosh* and *Tur* rule that only *Amen* and the seven words of *Yehei Shmei Rabbah* are recited (*Bais Yosef* 56). Vilna Gaon and Magen Avraham (to 56:3) follow this ruling because יִתְבָּרַךְ [*Yisborach*], *may He be blessed*, begins a new thought which is unrelated to the earlier one.

(b) *Orach Chaim* 56:3 and the Kabbalists [cited by *Aruch HaShulchan* 56:4] maintain that the word *Yisborach* should be added to the *Yehei Shmei Rabbah* response. This is based on the *Midrash* [see footnote] which declares that it is a major transgression to interrupt between the words עָלְמַיָא and יִתְבָּרַךְ.[1]

This *Midrash* (see footnote) seems to contradict the view cited above (a) that *Yisborach* is not said. Those commentators, however, maintain that although the congregation is not to say *Yisborach*, the *Midrash* teaches that the people must listen to the *chazzan's* continuation of *Yisborach* without speaking or any other interruption. The *chazzan*, too, is thereby cautioned not to pause excessively.

(c) *Bais Yosef*, citing a *siddur* of *Gaonim* (*Tur* 56), maintains that the proper response is to recite all twenty-eight words from *Yehei Shmei Rabbah*

until דְּאֲמִירָן בְּעָלְמָא. This will allude to all the implications of the number twenty-eight as cited above.

Since all three opinions are strongly supported, any of the customs is equally valid. However, according to the first opinion, the recitation of anything after עָלְמַיָא would constitute a forbidden interruption when said during portions of the *tefillah* where extraneous speech is not permitted. Therefore, if one hears *Kaddish* during his own *tefillah* at a point where he would be forbidden to answer *Amen*, but *is* permitted to interrupt for *Amen Yehei Shemei Rabbah*, he should stop at עָלְמַיָא and *not* continue with *Yisborach* (*Chaye Adam*; *Mishneh Berurah* 56 §15).

**7.** יִתְבָּרַךְ — *Blessed ... be.*

This is the first of eight terms of praise. They continue the theme that, in time to come, God will be acknowledged and extolled by all mankind, and that His praises will go beyond all blessings and songs that are uttered in the world (*Emek Brachah*).

R' Yehudah ben Yakar, Abudraham and other early and later commentators cite various Scriptural verses as bases for each of these eight expressions of praise.

[It is interesting to note the general agreement that וְיִתְפָּאַר, *may He take pride*, is based on יִשְׂרָאֵל אֲשֶׁר בְּךָ אֶתְפָּאָר, *Israel, for in you I*

---

1. *Bais Yosef* cites the following *Midrash*:

R' Elazar ben R' Yose said: Once when I was traveling I met Elijah and with him were four thousand laden camels. I asked him, 'With what are they laden?' He answered, 'With anger and wrath!

What for?

To take vengeance with anger and wrath from those who converse between *Kaddish* and *Borchu*, between blessing [of *Shmoneh Esrei*] and blessing, between chapter [of the *Sh'ma*] and chapter, and between *Amen Yehei Shmei Rabbah* and *Yisborach*.'

**7** *Blessed, lauded, glorified, extolled,*
*upraised, honored, elevated, and praised*
*Be the Name of the Holy One,*
*Blessed be He —* Congregation responds: *Blessed be He.*
(Some respond: *Amen*).

take pride or glory [Isaiah 49:3].
God declares that His source of
pride in the universe is Israel. As
His chosen nation, Israel provides
God with glory, as it were, by carry-
ing out His wishes. Even at the End
of Days, when all nations will
recognize God, He will still pride
Himself in the virtuous behavior of
His People.]

**◄§ Vocalization of יִתְבָּרַךְ, etc.**
The vocalization of the next group of
words is subject to the same dispute as
the first two words of *Kaddish*. We
have given the *Aramaic* vocalization as
required by *R' Yaakov Emden* and
*Avodas Yisrael* who maintain that the
root words of this group are the same in
Aramaic as they are in Hebrew.
Therefore, since the rest of the *Kaddish*
was rendered in Aramaic these words,
too, should follow that pattern.
*Abudraham* and *Bais Yoseif,*
however, maintain that these words are
Hebrew, and explain that they were not
translated into Aramaic because there
were no adequate translations in that
language. If so, the vocalization should
be as follows: יִתְבָּרֵךְ וְיִשְׁתַּבַח וְיִתְפָּאֵר
וְיִתְרוֹמֵם.[1]

**וְיִתְהַלָּל — And praised be.**
*Siddur Bais Yaakov* comments
that this praise refers to the fear of

God [i.e. God's praise is found in
the fact that His creatures stand in
awe of Him].
*Vilna Gaon* omits this word
because this section of *Kaddish*
should contain only seven words of
praise as an allusion to the seven
heavens. [For an explanation of the
symbolism see "Numerical significance of *Yehei Shmei Rabbah*"
above.] Since וְיִתְהַלָּל would be the
*eighth*, and hence incongruous
word, it should be omitted.
*HaManhig,* citing *R' Amram*
comments that according to the
custom that *Yisborach* is attached to
*Yehei Shmei Rabbah,* that word is
counted as part of this section, with
the result that וְיִתְהַלָּל is, indeed, the
seventh word.

**שְׁמֵהּ דְּקֻדְשָׁא בְּרִיךְ הוּא — *The Name***
*of the Holy One, Blessed be He.*
The translation follows *Rambam,*
*Abudraham, Vilna Gaon, Mor*
*U'Ketziah, Shaarei Teshuvah* and
*Mishnah Berurah.* Thus rendered,
the term קֻדְשָׁא בְּרִיךְ הוּא is simply
the Aramaic equivalent of the fam-
iliar appellation הַקָּדוֹשׁ בָּרוּךְ הוּא, *the*
*Holy One, Blessed be He.*
*Or Zarua, Rama, Magen Av-*
*raham* and *Avodas Yisrael* comment

---

1. [It should be noted that the English translations of such words of praise cannot be more
than approximate. As the Sages taught, ancient Roman is a language of war, Greek is a
language of art, and Hebrew, the Holy Tongue, is a language of holiness.
Each people develops words to express the concepts it holds dear; therefore the nature of a
people can be gauged, to some extent, by the range of expression it had developed for particular ideas. The Roman Empire had a passion for war, so it had an unmatched range of expression to convey concepts related to the martial arts. Israel is the nation of holiness,
therefore it has a spiritual vocabulary expressing delicate nuances that are not found in the
lexicons of other peoples. Indeed, this is one reason why Hebrew is called לְשׁוֹן הַקֹּדֶשׁ, literally,
the Language of Holiness.]

that שְׁמֵהּ דְקֻדְשָׁא is the end of one section and בְּרִיךְ הוּא begins the next. Accordingly, they punctuate and render as follows: וְיִתְהַלָּל שְׁמֵהּ דְקֻדְשָׁא, *Praised be His Holy Name...* בְּרִיךְ הוּא לְעֵלָּא מִן כָּל בִּרְכָתָא..., *He is blessed beyond all blessings ...*

[It may be noted that the latter interpretation better follows the context of *Kaddish*. Throughout the prayer, the object of the praises has been the 'Name' of God, rather than God Himself.]

Although *Orach Chaim* 56:2 rules that the congregation responds *Amen* at this point, *Rama* notes that the customary response is בְּרִיךְ הוּא, *Blessed be He.*

[The intent of the response is that upon hearing mention of God's Name, the community answers that it is blessed. This is similar to בָּרוּךְ הוּא וּבָרוּךְ שְׁמוֹ, *Blessed be He and Blessed be His Name,* with which the congregation greets the *chazzan's* blessing of God. However, it is not considered an essential response, and may not be said during parts of the *tefillah* where interruptions are forbidden.]

*Ba'er Heitev* adds a caution to those who do not limit their response to the two words *B'rich Hu*. They should not say only בְּרִיךְ הוּא לְעֵילָּא, *Blessed be He above,* because this would carry the blasphemous implication that God is blessed only in Heaven above, but not on earth. Rather, if they prefer to extend the response, they should say בְּרִיךְ הוּא לְעֵילָּא מִן כָּל בִּרְכָתָא וְשִׁירָתָא, *Blessed is He beyond all blessing and songs.*

### ◆§ Ten Expressions of praise

[Ten expressions of praise are found in *Kaddish*: The first two words, יִתְגַּדַּל וְיִתְקַדֵּשׁ, and the eight words from יִתְבָּרֵךְ to וְיִתְהַלָּל. *Shibbolei HaLeket* deals with two aspects of this ten-fold praise: the symbolism of ten, and why the first two words are separated from the other eight.]

— The ten terms of praise allude to the Ten Utterances with which God created the universe (*Avos* 5:1). This is indicated by the second phrase of *Kaddish* which relates the desired exaltation and sanctification to the tangible world.

— The ten terms allude further to the Ten Commandments, for the Sages teach that the utterances with which the world was created are directly related to the commandments (*Pesikta Rabbasi* 21). [The implication is that the world was created for the sake of His precepts; God created the universe as the setting for the performance of His will, and human beings give meaning to creation by fulfilling His wishes.]

— The praises of *Kaddish* are divided into sets of two and eight because the Ten Commandments were given in two sets. God transmitted the first two directly to Israel while the last eight were given Israel by Moses (*Makkos* 24a).

— The *Midrash* teaches that in time to come, God will don ten garments, as it were, and wreak vengeance on the ten nations listed in *Psalms* 83, who subjugated Israel.

— *Gesher HaChaim* adds that they refer to the *Ten Sefiros*, the emanations through which God's influence filters from His realm to human consciousness.

*Ravan*, however, finds *fifteen* expressions of praise in *Kaddish*: the ten mentioned above, plus וְיַמְלִיךְ מַלְכוּתֵהּ, *and [may He] establish His kingdom,* and the four expressions in stich 6. He comments that they allude to the fifteen Songs of Ascents [*Psalms* 120-134].

*Eliyahu Rabbah* comments that fifteen alludes to the numerical value of God's Name יָהּ [the letters with which God created heaven and earth and, according to some commentators noted above (s.v. שְׁמֵהּ רַבָּא), the Name used in *Kaddish*].

*Beyond all blessings, songs, praises, and consolations*
*that are uttered on earth.   Now respond: Amen.*

Congregation responds: *Amen.*

*[This point marks the completion of Half Kaddish.]*

---

**8.** לְעֵלָּא מִן כָּל בִּרְכָתָא — *Beyond* [lit. *above*] *all blessings.*

May God be praised and exalted far beyond all the *blessings, songs, praises,* and *consolations* of the prophets, for no matter how perceptive, eloquent, and inspired a human being is, he cannot do justice to the greatness of God (*Shibbolei HaLeket*).

[Although the words of the prophets were given them by God, they must of necessity fall short of a true description of God's essence simply because the words are filtered through human intelligence and limited by human vocabulary. Just as words cannot fully convey an emotion or a vision, they can surely not define God's greatness.]

*R' Yehudah ben Yakar* and *Abudraham* interpret differently. The praises mentioned here are not prophetic ones referring to God, but praises lauding human kings and heroes. Thus, God is described as far above any humanly imagined expressions of praise.

לְעֵלָּא לְעֵלָּא — *Exceedingly beyond* [lit. *beyond, beyond*].

During עֲשֶׂרֶת יְמֵי תְּשׁוּבָה, *the Ten Days of Repentance* [from *Rosh HaShanah* to *Yom Kippur*], the word לְעֵלָּא is repeated to stress that God's majesty is even more pronounced during this period of judgment than it is all year round.

Although some versions have a conjuctive ו, [וּלְעֵלָּא וּלְעֵלָּא] between the two words, most commentators agree that the *vav* is omitted, following the version favored by *Shibbolei HaLeket* for the year round *Kaddish. Emek Brachah* cites *Deuteronomy* 28:43 as the source of this double phrase. The term מַעְלָה מָעְלָה is rendered by *Onkelos* as לְעֵלָּא לְעֵלָּא, without a *vav*.

During the Ten Days of Repentance, the two words מִן כָּל are contracted into the single word מִכָּל. This is done to keep the total number of words in the final section at twenty-eight in line with the symbolism described above.

וְשִׁירָתָא — *[And] songs.*

[Throughout Scripture, God is praised in 'song' at times when people become aware to an unusual degree that all of the infinite and seemingly unrelated and contradictory facets of existence actually move in harmony toward the attainment of His goals. This concept is discussed at length in the Overview to *Shir HaShirim.* The various songs in Scripture are described by the Sages as representing differing degrees of such perception. The song of *Numbers* 21:17-20, because it was sung after Israel's sins had caused Moses to lose the privilege of leading them into *Eretz Yisrael*, lacked the inspiration of Moses and therefore, the Sages teach, was inferior to the Song of the Sea. The greater the perception, the greater the song. Here the *Kaddish* proclaims that when the final Redemption comes, human recognition of the harmony of creation in the service of God will be such that even the *songs* of history's greatest moments will be inadequate to express the newly acquired perception of God's greatness.]

וְנֶחֱמָתָא — *And consolations.*

The books of the Prophets are filled with visions of consolation, comforting Israel with the knowledge that its exile will be followed

⁹ תִּתְקַבֵּל צְלוֹתְהוֹן וּבָעוּתְהוֹן דְּכָל בֵּית

by redemption. But, as the Talmud (*Berachos* 34b) teaches, the reality of life after the Redemption will be so great that עַיִן לֹא רָאָתָה, *no eye* — not even the most elevated prophetic eye — *has seen* a degree of greatness equivalent to the reality (*Aruch HaShulchan*).[1]

There are two other interpretations:

— *Gesher HaChaim* and *R' Munk* cite a view that the word comes from the Arabic word for glorification or praise.

— *R' Munk* cites *Targum* to *Joel* 2:14 which renders מִנְחָה, *offering* as נֶחָמָן.

*Shibbolei HaLeket*, quoting *Rashi*, comments that the three words וְשִׁירָתָא תֻּשְׁבְּחָתָא וְנֶחָמָתָא go together:

God's greatness will be acknowledged to a degree beyond all the songs of praise [שִׁירָתָא וְתֻשְׁבְּחָתָא] that King David composed to be recited on the day when God will bring נֶחָמָתָא, *consolations*, to Israel through the final Redemption. The reality of the Redemption will be even greater than that envisioned by the prophets.

דַּאֲמִירָן בְּעָלְמָא — *That are uttered on earth.*

According to the interpretation given above on the preceding phrase of *Kaddish*, this refers to the prophetic praises and consolations that are uttered on earth.

[In a similar vein, we may interpret this term as a reference to the *hiddenness* of earthly existence, as described above in stich 6 s.v. לְעָלַם. In our current spiritual state when so much of God's greatness is obscured, we cannot hope to understand the true extent of God's greatness. Only later, when God reveals His splendor will we be able to exalt and sanctify Him adequately.]

According to *R' Yehudah ben Yakar* and *Abudraham*, however, this means simply the praises uttered on earth in praise of human dignitaries.

### ⋖§ End of Half Kaddish

This point marks the end of חֲצִי קַדִּישׁ, *the Half Kaddish*. It should be borne in mind, however, that the popular term *Half Kaddish* is a misnomer; the previous eight stiches are halachically and historically the entire *Kaddish*. The additional stiches, 9-11 for the *chazzan* and 10-11 for mourners, are later additions to the basic text of *Kaddish*. The titles *Full Kaddish* and *Mourner's Kaddish* are convenient for purposes of identification, but they should not be taken to imply that the so-called *Half Kaddish* is deficient in any way.

This discussion has *halachic* implications. Since the following stiches are not parts of the essential *Kaddish*, listeners may not respond

1. *Abudraham* understands the word as a new prayer that God find consolation. Since He grieves at the exile and oppression of Israel, we pray that He find comfort in the Redemption and success of His People. This concept is based on the following passage in *Berachos* 3a:

Whenever Jews enter synagogues and study halls and declare, 'May His great Name be blessed [*Yehei Shmei Rabbah*]...', the Holy One, Blessed be He, nods His head and says, 'Fortunate is the King Who is praised in His home in this manner! Why did the Father have to exile His children! Woe to the children who were exiled from their Father's table.'

### ⁹ *May the prayers and supplications of the entire Family of Israel*

*Amen* during prayers where it is forbidden to interrupt for an ordinary *Amen.*

[In some communities it is customary for the congregation to precede each of the last three stiches with a verse of prayer or praise. These verses, given above in the text of *Kaddish*, are recited only during the *Full Kaddish* of the *chazzan*. I have been unable to find the source of this custom. Respectively these added verses are from שְׁמַע קוֹלֵנוּ, *Hear our voice*, of the weekday *Shemoneh Esrei; Psalms* 113:2, and *Psalms* 121:2.]

**9.** [Mourners omit this stich. (See introduction to Mourner's *Kaddish*.)]

תִּתְקַבֵּל — *May ... be accepted.*

This stich is a plea for God's acceptance of the community's just-completed prayers. It is recited after *Shemoneh Esrei* and *Selichos*. During the weekday *Shacharis*, this plea for acceptance of our prayers is delayed until after וּבָא לְצִיּוֹן גּוֹאֵל, *May the Redeemer come to Zion,* which is the conclusion of the essential section of the morning's prayers.

[As noted above, the Aramaic vocalization would be תִּתְקַבַּל, whereas the Hebrew would be תִּתְקַבֵּל. Strangely, most of the communities which use the Aramaic vocalization of יִתְגַּדַּל וְיִתְקַדַּשׁ earlier, have adopted the Hebrew vocalization here. The exception is the German community which is consistent in using the Aramaic vocalization throughout.]

צְלוֹתְהוֹן וּבָעוּתְהוֹן — *The[ir] prayers and the[ir] supplications.*

The phrase is based on the *Targum* of Jacob's description of his conquest of Shechem. He referred to the city as the place אֲשֶׁר לָקַחְתִּי מִיַּד הָאֱמֹרִי בְּחַרְבִּי וּבְקַשְׁתִּי, *which I took from the hand of the Amorite with my sword and my bow (Genesis 48:22). Onkelos* renders the phrase 'with my sword and my bow' as בִּצְלוֹתִי וּבְבָעוּתִי, *with my prayer and my supplication.* [Thus, the use of this phrase recalls the merit of the Patriarch] *(R' Yehudah ben Yakar; Abudraham).*

*Avodas Yisrael* and *Emek Brachah* cite the more direct source: וְשָׁמַעְתָּ הַשָּׁמַיִם אֶת תְּפִלָּתָם וְאֵת תְּחִנָּתָם, *May You hear in heaven their prayer and their supplication (I Kings 8:45),* which *Targum* renders as יַת צְלוֹתְהוֹן וְיַת בָּעוּתְהוֹן.

*Harchev Davar* to *Genesis* 48:22 explains the difference between תְּפִלָּה, *prayer,* and תְּחִנָּה, *supplication.* Prayer is the set, unchanging prayer that the Sages formulated for all people. Supplication is the individual plea for personal needs. Such pleas may be inserted into relevant parts of the *Shemoneh Esrei,* or one may have them in mind as he recites the general prayer. For example, when reciting the blessing pertaining to health [רְפָאֵנוּ], which contains the general prayer that all illness be healed, one may insert a plea for an individual patient. Similarly, though someone recites only the standard text of *tefillah,* he will generally have personal needs in mind.[1]

1. Jacob described his תְּפִלָּה, [set] *prayer,* as a *sword,* but his תְּחִנָּה, [individual] *supplication,* as a *bow.* Why the difference?

  The efficacy of these two forms of prayer varies. Whenever one recites Israel's universal

יִשְׂרָאֵל קֳדָם אֲבוּהוֹן דִּי בִשְׁמַיָּא. וְאִמְרוּ
אָמֵן: אמן

קהל: יְהֵי שֵׁם יהוה מְבֹרָךְ מֵעַתָּה וְעַד עוֹלָם:

10 יְהֵא שְׁלָמָא רַבָּא מִן שְׁמַיָּא. וְחַיִּים (טוֹבִים).
עָלֵינוּ וְעַל כָּל יִשְׂרָאֵל. וְאִמְרוּ אָמֵן: אמן

---

דְּכָל בֵּית יִשְׂרָאֵל — *Of the entire Family* [lit. *house*] *of Israel.*

[As is common, prayers are given a communal nature; they are said on behalf of the nation, rather than the individual. We ask, therefore, that the prayers and supplications of the *entire Family of Israel* be accepted. In contrast to the early portion of *Kaddish* where special second person mention was made of the congregants with whom the reader is praying — בְּחַיֵּיכוֹן, *in your lifetime* — the text here is only general, and not particular. This is due to the differing nature of the two parts of *Kaddish*. Earlier, the prime purpose of the reader's words was to elicit the *Yehei Shmei Rabbah* response from the congregation (see *comm.* above and Overview), therefore the reader's plea is directed to the listeners as well as the general community. The final verses of *Kaddish*, however, are additional prayers of a general nature, therefore, they follow the usual third-person formula of prayer.]

אֲבוּהוֹן דִּי בִשְׁמַיָּא — *Their Father Who is in Heaven.*

This title for God is frequently found in Talmudic literature (*R' Yehudah ben Yakar*).

[When Moses was dispatched to Pharaoh to seek the release of Israel, his opening words in the name of God were בְּנִי בְכֹרִי יִשְׂרָאֵל, *My primary child is Israel* (*Exodus* 4:22). That was at a time when Israel was mired in the spiritual contamination of Egypt and when it was unworthy of redemption on its own merits. In describing Israel as His 'primary child,' God revealed a Father-son relationship that transcends sin and degradation. Similarly, the Talmud (*Taanis* 25b) records that on one occasion when prayers for rain were of no avail, R' Akiva stepped forward to lead the community. He began: אָבִינוּ מַלְכֵּנוּ אָבִינוּ אָתָּה, *Our Father, our King — You are our Father.* God has a dual relationship to Israel — Father and King. In the body of *Kaddish*, we prayed for the emergence of God as the universally acknowledged King of the universe. Now we add that He is our Father — and, therefore, He should accept our prayers though we are undeserving.

[*Or HaChaim* (*Deuteronomy* 26:15) explains that the term 'Heaven' represents God's sustaining and inspiring flow of spiritual and material influence. His will is fulfilled when people are worthy of receiving spiritual growth as well as material prosperity.

[Thus the term *Our Father in Heaven* may be understood as an implied plea that God have mercy on His wayward children and bring to fruition the full potential of His Heavenly blessings.]

prayer he has two important factors in his favor: The holiness of the prayer due to its formulation by such august personages as the Men of the Great Assembly, and the merit of the entire nation which recites the same text. Thus, even if his own concentration is lacking, the prayer can still be efficacious — like a sword, which, by virtue of the sharpness of its blade, can be effective even when it is not wielded well. But a personal prayer can be only as powerful as the devotion, concentration, and merit of the supplicant — like a bow which can dispatch an arrow tellingly only to the extent it is properly strung, supple, and stretched by the archer (*Rabbi Yitzchok Zev Soloveitchick*).

> *Be accepted before their Father*
> *Who is in Heaven.*     *Now respond: Amen.*
>
>                 Congregation responds: *Amen.*
>
> Congregation: *May the Name of HASHEM be blessed from now to eternity.*
> 10 *May there be abundant peace from Heaven,*
>      *and (good) life, upon us and upon all Israel.*
>                  *Now respond: Amen.*
>
>                 Congregation responds: *Amen.*

**10.** [Mourner's Kaddish resumes here]

יְהֵא שְׁלָמָא רַבָּא — *May there be abundant peace.*

The prayer for peace is the concluding one — as it is in *Shemoneh Esrei* and *Bircas HaMazon* — because peace is as important as all other blessings combined, since they are worthless unless they can be enjoyed in peace (*Abudraham*).[1]

*Emek Brachah* renders שְׁלָמָא רַבָּא as *abundant greeting*, i.e., may the heavenly spiritual forces be pleased with us and signify this by providing our needs graciously. One can meet his needs with aggravation and dread, or he can achieve the same earnings and benefits with ease and pleasure. May God provide for us a 'smiling countenance,' so to speak.

In support of his reluctance to adopt the more common translation, *Emek Brachah* comments that if *this* is a plea for peace, why

should the next verse again refer to peace?

מִן שְׁמַיָּא — *From Heaven.*

[Interpretations of this term's significance are found above. This may also be an acknowledgment that no matter what exertions are made in the political, military, diplomatic, and economic spheres, peace — the supreme necessity — is a heavenly gift. As the Sages teach, the heart of kings and rulers is in God's hand. We pray, therefore, that we be granted peace *from Heaven*, because we have seen too many aborted human attempts to achieve peace.]

וְחַיִּים — *And life.*

The wish for שְׁלָמָא רַבָּא, *abundant peace*, could be misconstrued since the expression *peace* can be used in connection with death, as in בְּשָׁלוֹם תָּמוּת, *you will die in peace* (*Jeremiah* 34:5). Therefore, after asking for peace, we add that we

---

1. *Abudraham* cites several Talmudic and Midrashic references in praise of peace:
Perhaps you will say, 'Here [are blessings of] food and drink, [but] without peace all is worthless!' Therefore the Torah says: *I will provide peace in the land* (*Leviticus* 26:6). This teaches that peace is equivalent to everything (*Toras Kohanim, Bechukosai* 1).

Peace is great. For the Holy One, Blessed be He, says of His great Name which was written with holiness, 'Let it be scraped [lit. erased] into the water to make peace between man and wife (*Chullin* 141a). [The *Talmud* refers to the case of a *Sotah*, a wife accused of infidelity. In order to establish her innocence, a written chapter of the Torah, containing Names which it is otherwise forbidden to erase, is scraped into water which she proceeds to drink. The procedure is given in *Numbers* Ch. 5.]

Peace is great, because the Torah is praised with the attribute of peace, as it is said: *and all its paths are peaceful* (*Proverbs* 3:17). Peace is great because even the celestial beings, who have no jealousy, hatred, or evil eye, need peace, as it is said (*Job* 25:2): *he makes peace in His heights* (*Bamidbar Rabbah* 11:7).

קהל: עֶזְרִי מֵעִם יהוה עֹשֵׂה שָׁמַיִם וָאָרֶץ:

11 עֹשֶׂה שָׁלוֹם (בעשי״ת: הַשָּׁלוֹם) בִּמְרוֹמָיו. הוּא
(בְּרַחֲמָיו) יַעֲשֶׂה שָׁלוֹם עָלֵינוּ וְעַל כָּל יִשְׂרָאֵל.
וְאִמְרוּ אָמֵן: אמן

want it to be in life, not death (Do-ver Shalom).

R' Yehudah ben Yakar gives as the source for the prayer for life, the passage from *Psalms* 21:5: חַיִּים שָׁאַל מִמְּךָ נָתַתָּה לּוֹ, *he asked life of You, You gave it to him.* Rashi interprets the verse as a reference to David's prayers for the privilege of living in *Eretz Yisrael* which is called (*Psalms* 116:9) אַרְצוֹת הַחַיִּים, *lands of the living.* Thus, we may interpret this part of *Kaddish* as a prayer for the coming of the Messiah when all Israel will return to its land. Indeed, since *Kaddish* is a prayer for maximum sanctification of God's Name, the holiness of *Eretz Yisrael* is an important factor in achieving the purpose of *Kaddish.*

טוֹבִים — *Good.*

[This adjective is added in *Nusach Sfard.*] Unless life is good, of what use is it? (*R' Yehudah ben Yakar*).

◆§ **Three steps backward**

At this point, the reader bows like a servant taking leave from his master (*Orach Chaim* 123:1, *Mishneh Berurah*) and, while bowing, takes three steps backward. This follows the practice of stepping backward at the conclusion of *Shemoneh Esrei* when this verse is recited. Various reasons are given for the three steps. Some are the following:

— When one prays before God, the place where he stands becomes holy and the *Shechinah* [Divine Presence] rests over him. Upon concluding his prayer, he steps out of the holy place, as it were (*Shibbolei HaLeket*).

— The daily prayers are like sacrificial offerings. When the priests left the altar, they had to step across three rows of stones to reach the ramp back to the courtyard (*R' Hai Gaon*).

— The Sages teach [see *Maharsha, Sanhedrin* 96a] that Nebuchadnezzar took three steps in honor of God, and thereby earned the right to destroy the Temple. In response, we take three steps to pay honor to God's Presence (*Mishnah Berurah* 123 n. 2). [In the case of *Shemoneh Esrei*, this allusion is carried forward by a prayer שֶׁיִּבָּנֶה בֵּית הַמִּקְדָּשׁ, *that the Holy Temple be built.* This is equally applicable to *Kaddish* which has been a prayer for the sanctification of God's Name which will include the building of the Temple.]

After having gone three steps backward, the reader bows to his left, saying עֹשֶׂה שָׁלוֹם בִּמְרוֹמָיו, *He Who makes peace in His heights;* bows to his right, saying הוּא יַעֲשֶׂה שָׁלוֹם עָלֵינוּ, *may He make peace upon us;* then bows straight ahead and completes *Kaddish.* It is as if God stands before us: when we first bow leftward, we bow to His right, the side which is always honored first (*Bais Yoseif* 123).

R' Munk comments that the bow to God's right (our left) symbolizes God's spirit of Mercy, represented by the angel Michael who stands at the right of God's throne. The bow to God's left (our right) symbolizes His spirit of punishing justice, represented by the angel Gabriel, who stands to the left of the throne. Finally we bow forward, to God Himself, acknowledging that only He resolves all conflicts and unifies all forces in the universe.

**11.** עֹשֶׂה שָׁלוֹם בִּמְרוֹמָיו — *He Who makes peace in His heights.*

This appellation for God is found

11 *He Who makes (the) peace in His heights,*
*may He (in His Mercy) make peace upon us,*
*and upon all Israel.* Now respond: *Amen.*

in Job 25:2. *Rashi* and *Ibn Ezra* there explain that the various heavenly forces often appear to contradict one another, such as angels of mercy and angels of judgment. Nevertheless God creates harmony above so that all the powers and qualities function harmoniously in obedience to His Will.

'Peace,' in the sense of this verse, is God's implication of harmony upon the various forces with the result that each power functions within the bounds assigned it, and without interference from others (*Etz Yosef* to *Shemoneh Esrei*).

[For example, there is a delicate balance between night and day; between tropical, temperate, and frigid temperatures. If the earth were too close to the sun or too far, life could not exist. There are endless instances of cosmic forces which interact so as to further God's ends — the peace He imposes on high.]

עֹשֶׂה הַשָּׁלוֹם — *He Who makes the peace.*

In some communities, this version — הַשָּׁלוֹם, **the** *peace* — is said during the Ten Days of Repentance because the word הַשָּׁלוֹם has the numerical value of 381, equal to that of סַפְרִיאֵל, *Safriel*, the angel who counts merits and sins. Thus it is particularly relevant to the period when people's deeds are being counted and evaluated (*Mateh Ephraim* 582:1). Most commentators, however, either ignore the custom or oppose it. *Kaf HaChaim (O. Ch.* 56:38) cites an opinion that this formula should be used in the last blessing of *Shemoneh Esrei* dur-

ing the Days of Awe, but *never* during *Kaddish*, because the last stich of *Kaddish* is based on a Scriptural verse (*Job* 25:2), and should not be tampered with. He concludes, however, that הַשָּׁלוֹם may be said by the *chazzan*, in a *Kaddish* following *Shemoneh Esrei*, but it should be omitted in other recitations.

הוּא יַעֲשֶׂה שָׁלוֹם עָלֵינוּ — *May He make peace upon us.*

If the Heavenly forces require God to make peace among them, surely human beings who are so prone to jealousy, hatred, and fractious conduct require God's mercy to bring peaceful harmony into their relationship (*Etz Yosef*).

בְּרַחֲמָיו — *In His mercy.*

This word is included according to *Rambam* and Sephardic *siddurim*; however, it is omitted in all Ashkenazic versions, except in *Kaddish D'Rabbanan*. This custom may be based on *Sotah* 49a where the Sages teach that the survival of the universe depends on the *Kaddish* recited after the teachings of the rabbis, and that each succeeding day is progressively more accursed since the destruction of the Temple. Since this particular *Kaddish* is so vital to the very survival of an afflicted world, a plea for mercy is particularly apt at this point (*Emek Brachah*).

וְעַל כָּל יִשְׂרָאֵל — *And upon all Israel.*

[The concluding verse of *Kaddish* asks for peace upon the entire nation. As the Sages teach in the very last words of the *Mishnah*: The Holy One, Blessed be He, found no

יִתְגַּדַּל וְיִתְקַדַּשׁ שְׁמֵהּ רַבָּא. אמן

בְּעָלְמָא דִּי בְרָא כִרְעוּתֵהּ. וְיַמְלִיךְ

מַלְכוּתֵהּ. (וְיַצְמַח פֻּרְקָנֵהּ וִיקָרֵב מְשִׁיחֵהּ. אמן) בְּחַיֵּיכוֹן

וּבְיוֹמֵיכוֹן וּבְחַיֵּי דְכָל בֵּית יִשְׂרָאֵל. בַּעֲגָלָא

וּבִזְמַן קָרִיב. וְאִמְרוּ אָמֵן: אמן

יְהֵא שְׁמֵהּ רַבָּא מְבָרַךְ לְעָלַם וּלְעָלְמֵי

עָלְמַיָּא:

יִתְבָּרַךְ וְיִשְׁתַּבַּח וְיִתְפָּאַר וְיִתְרוֹמַם וְיִתְנַשֵּׂא

וְיִתְהַדָּר וְיִתְעַלֶּה וְיִתְהַלָּל שְׁמֵהּ דְּקֻדְשָׁא בְּרִיךְ

הוּא. בריך הוא [אמן]

לְעֵלָּא מִן כָּל (בעשי"ת: לְעֵלָּא לְעֵלָּא מִכָּל) בִּרְכָתָא

וְשִׁירָתָא תֻּשְׁבְּחָתָא וְנֶחֱמָתָא. דַּאֲמִירָן בְּעָלְמָא.

וְאִמְרוּ אָמֵן: אמן

יְהֵא שְׁלָמָא רַבָּא מִן שְׁמַיָּא. וְחַיִּים (טובים).

עָלֵינוּ וְעַל כָּל יִשְׂרָאֵל. וְאִמְרוּ אָמֵן: אמן

עֹשֶׂה שָׁלוֹם (בעשי"ת: הַשָּׁלוֹם) בִּמְרוֹמָיו. הוּא

(בְּרַחֲמָיו) יַעֲשֶׂה שָׁלוֹם עָלֵינוּ וְעַל כָּל יִשְׂרָאֵל.

וְאִמְרוּ אָמֵן: אמן

vessel so able to contain blessing for Israel as peace, as it is written, (*Psalms* 29:11): HASHEM *will give* might *to His nation,* HASHEM *will bless His nation with peace* (Uktzin 3:12).]

### ﬞﬞﬞ קַדִּישׁ יָתוֹם / Mourner's Kaddish

For the eleven months following the death of a parent, a son is obligated to recite *Kaddish* as a source of merit for the soul of the departed. [For a discussion of the concept and the basis for the practice, see *Overview.*] This *Kaddish* is also recited on the *yahrzeit* [anniversary of the death].

This *Kaddish* is identical with the *Full Kaddish* except that stich 9, which applies only to the *chazzan* praying for acceptance of the congregation's service, does not apply to a mourner and

# ৵§ Mourner's Kaddish

M ay His great Name be exalted and sanctified
                    Congregation responds: *Amen.*
    in the world He created according to His will;
And may He establish His Kingship
    (and cause His salvation to sprout and bring near
    His Messiah —         Congregation responds: *Amen.*)
During your lifetime and during your days
    and during the lifetime of the entire
    Family of Israel,
Swiftly and soon.         Now respond: Amen.
                    Congregation responds: *Amen.*

Congregation responds aloud with the following stich, and *chazzan* repeats:

May His great Name be blessed forever and ever.

Blessed, lauded, glorified, extolled,
    upraised, honored, elevated, and praised
Be the Name of the Holy One,
    Blessed be He —    Congregation responds: *Blessed be He.*
                    (Some respond: *Amen*).

(During Ten Days of Repentance: *Exceedingly*)
Beyond all blessings, songs, praises, and consolations
    that are uttered on earth.   Now respond: Amen.
                    Congregation responds: *Amen.*
May there be abundant peace from Heaven,
    and (good) life, upon us and upon all Israel.
                    Now respond: Amen.
                    Congregation responds: *Amen.*
He Who makes (the) peace in His heights,
    may He (in His Mercy) make peace upon us,
    and upon all Israel.   Now respond: Amen.
                    Congregation responds: *Amen.*

is therefore omitted from the *Mourner's Kaddish*. The full text and translation are presented here for the convenience of the reader. For commentary, see above, 'Half and Full Kaddish.'

# קַדִּישׁ דְּרַבָּנָן

**יִתְגַּדַּל** וְיִתְקַדַּשׁ שְׁמֵהּ רַבָּא. אמן
בְּעָלְמָא דִּי בְרָא כִרְעוּתֵהּ. וְיַמְלִיךְ
מַלְכוּתֵהּ. (וְיַצְמַח פֻּרְקָנֵהּ וִיקָרֵב מְשִׁיחֵהּ. אמן) בְּחַיֵּיכוֹן
וּבְיוֹמֵיכוֹן וּבְחַיֵּי דְכָל בֵּית יִשְׂרָאֵל. בַּעֲגָלָא
וּבִזְמַן קָרִיב. וְאִמְרוּ אָמֵן: אמן

יְהֵא שְׁמֵהּ רַבָּא מְבָרַךְ לְעָלַם וּלְעָלְמֵי
עָלְמַיָּא:

יִתְבָּרַךְ וְיִשְׁתַּבַּח וְיִתְפָּאַר וְיִתְרוֹמַם וְיִתְנַשֵּׂא
וְיִתְהַדָּר וְיִתְעַלֶּה וְיִתְהַלָּל שְׁמֵהּ דְּקֻדְשָׁא בְּרִיךְ
הוּא. בריך הוא [אמן]

לְעֵלָּא מִן כָּל (בעשי״ת: לְעֵלָּא לְעֵלָּא מִכָּל) בִּרְכָתָא
וְשִׁירָתָא תֻּשְׁבְּחָתָא וְנֶחֱמָתָא. דַּאֲמִירָן בְּעָלְמָא.
וְאִמְרוּ אָמֵן: אמן

עַל יִשְׂרָאֵל וְעַל רַבָּנָן. וְעַל תַּלְמִידֵיהוֹן וְעַל
כָּל תַּלְמִידֵי תַלְמִידֵיהוֹן. וְעַל כָּל מָאן דְּעָסְקִין

## קַדִּישׁ דְּרַבָּנָן / The Rabbis' Kaddish

'Whenever ten or more Israelites engage in the study of the Oral Law — for example, *Mishnah, Halachah,* and even *Midrash* or *Aggadah* — one of them recites the *Rabbis' Kaddish* [upon conclusion of the study] (*Rambam, Nusach HaKaddish*). Although *Rambam* implies that this *Kaddish* is recited primarily after halachic portions of the Oral Law and only incidentally after the study of *Midrashic* teaching, many commentators maintain that it is said only after *Midrash.* This is based on *Sotah* 49a which speaks of יְהֵא שְׁמֵהּ רַבָּא דְּאַגַּדְתָּא, *Yehei Shmei Rabbah* [which is recited following the public teaching of] *Aggadah*, indicating that this *Kaddish* has special relevance to *Aggadic* [i.e., *Midrashic*] teaching. Therefore, *Magen Avraham* (54 §3) rules that a brief *Aggadic* passage should be taught after halachic study in order to qualify for the recitation of this *Kaddish.*

The distinctive feature of the *Kaddish* is the paragraph containing a prayer for the welfare of the rabbis, students, and the people who support their study. In the text of the prayer, Israel is named first, out of respect for the nation and because Moses, too, gave first mention to those who provide the necessary support for those who study Torah. In *Deuteronomy* 33:18, Moses referred to the partnership of Zevulun, the supporter of scholars, and Issachar, the scholarly tribe. He blessed Zevulun first.

This special prayer for members of the Torah community was appended only to study of the Oral — but not the Written — Law, because that part of the Torah, in particular, was left for the Sages to teach, expound, and study. Historically, the transmission of the Oral Law depended on the teacher-student relationship and tradition, hence the prayer for their welfare.

# ◆§ Rabbis' Kaddish

M ay His great Name be exalted and sanctified

Congregation responds: Amen.

in the world He created according to His will;
And may He establish His Kingship
(and cause His salvation to sprout and bring near
His Messiah) —          Congregation responds: Amen.)
During your lifetime and during your days
and during the lifetime of the entire
Family of Israel,
Swiftly and soon.          Now respond: Amen.

Congregation responds: Amen.

Congregation responds aloud with the following stich, and chazzan repeats:

May His great Name be blessed forever and ever.

Blessed, lauded, glorified, extolled,
upraised, honored, elevated, and praised
Be the Name of the Holy One,
Blessed be He —          Congregation responds: Blessed be He.
(Some respond: Amen).

(During Ten Days of Repentance: Exceedingly)
Beyond all blessings, songs, praises, and consolations
that are uttered on earth.          Now respond: Amen.

Congregation responds: Amen.

Upon Israel, upon the teachers,
their disciples and all their disciples' disciples,

---

With the exception of the special prayer for the Torah community, this *Kaddish* is identical to the *Mourner's Kaddish*. For commentary to this *Kaddish*, see *Full Kaddish* above.

עַל יִשְׂרָאֵל — *Upon Israel.*

Although this is a prayer for the benefit of the Torah community, it begins with mention of Israel. Any prayer for those who study Torah is, in reality, a prayer for all Israel since the spiritual welfare of the na-

tion depends on Torah study (R' Hirsch).

Unlike other parts of *Kaddish*, here we do not say כָּל, **all** of Israel, because subdivisions of the nation — teachers and students — are specified later. The connotation of

בְּאוֹרַיְתָא. דִּי בְאַתְרָא הָדֵין וְדִי בְּכָל אֲתַר
וַאֲתַר.
יְהֵא לְהוֹן וּלְכוֹן שְׁלָמָא רַבָּא. חִנָּא וְחִסְדָּא
וְרַחֲמִין. וְחַיִּין אֲרִיכִין. וּמְזוֹנֵי רְוִיחֵי. וּפֻרְקָנָא

this opening term, therefore, is the *rest* of Israel, which benefits from and supports the work of those who dedicate themselves to Torah study (*Emek Brachah*).

וְעַל רַבָּנָן — *Upon the teachers.*
[Although רַבָּנָן is commonly, and correctly, translated *rabbis*, it should be borne in mind that, whatever other functions they may have had, the rabbis were teachers of Torah. It is their role as transmitters of the Oral Law from one generation to the next that is the *leitmotif* of this prayer. The teachers and students are listed separately because they represent the two halves of the tradition by which Torah knowledge was communicated. Because the Oral Law was not to be committed to writing, the scholarship, personality, methodology, character, and life style of teachers could be communicated in the process of relaying knowledge. This, too, was of the essence of the Oral Law. (See introduction to *Kiryas Sefer; Resisei Laylah* 56).]

We do not say כָּל רַבָּנָן, **all** *the teachers*, because the word כָּל, *all,* was omitted above with reference to Israel. To use the word now after having omitted it earlier would seem demeaning to Israel (*Emek Brachah*).

תַּלְמִידֵיהוֹן — *Their disciples.*
[We have chosen to render *disciples* rather than *students,* because disciples contains the connotation of dedicated adherence to a teaching

or doctrine. The traditional chain of Torah scholarship demands this sort of relationship between student and teacher.]

כָּל תַּלְמִידֵי תַלְמִידֵיהוֹן — *All their disciples' disciples.*
Here the word כָּל, *all,* is included because that all-inclusive adjective is meant to imply that our prayer extends even to the youngest and most insignificant student of Torah (*Emek Brachah*).

כָּל מָאן דְּעָסְקִין בְּאוֹרַיְתָא — *All those who engage in [the study of] Torah.*
[I.e., those who are neither teachers nor students, but dedicate themselves to personal study. The use of כָּל, *all,* extends the prayer to anyone who studies Torah, no matter what the degree.]

דִּי בְאַתְרָא הָדֵין וְדִי בְּכָל אֲתַר וַאֲתַר — *Who are here or anywhere else* [lit. *in this place and in every place and place*].
[The separate references to the various places implies that each individual town and neighborhood benefits from the Torah study of its own citizens. While the activity of scholars benefits the entire nation, it is of particular advantage to the locale where it takes place.]
The place references refer not to the Torah, but to those who study and teach, and to Israel — wherever they may be (*Iyun Tefillah*).

יְהֵא לְהוֹן וּלְכוֹן — *May they and you have* [lit. *may there be to them and to you*].

*And upon all those who engage in the study of Torah,*
*who are here or anywhere else:*
*May they and you have abundant peace,*
*grace, kindness, and mercy,*
*Long life, ample nourishment, and salvation*

This version is found in virtually all *siddurim* and is the one in most common use. It expresses the wish that the blessings to be enumerated below may rest upon *them*, the people enumerated above, and *you*, the members of the congregation.

However, *R' Yaakov Emden, Avodas Yisrael*, and *Emek Brachah* dispute the authenticity of the version. *Avodas Yisrael* contends that it is foreign to the accepted style of prayer to go from third-person to second and then back to third-person. *Emek Brachah* argues that by saying *they and you*, the reader, in effect, excludes himself from the prayer.

*Avodas Yisrael* excludes לְכוֹן, *you* and reads only לְהוֹן, *they*. Accordingly, the reader refers to all the categories he has mentioned at least one of which includes himself. *Emek Brachah* prefers the version used by *R' Yaakov Emden* in his *siddur*: לְהוֹן וְלָנָא, *they and we* [lit. *to them and to us*].

שְׁלָמָא רַבָּא — *Abundant peace.*
This term appears near the end of the regular *Kaddish* and was discussed there. *Emek Brachah* comments that it would appear redundant to pray for *abundant peace* in this paragraph and then repeat the identical phrase in the next verse. He notes that *R' Yaakov Emden* omits the word רַבָּא, *abundant*, and that the word does not appear in *Rambam's* text either. Therefore, he maintains that here we should ask only for שְׁלָמָא, *peace*, and leave the word רַבָּא, *abundant*, for the next stich. Thus, although we will be repeating the request for peace, we

will be adding a new, intensifying element in the form of רַבָּא, **abundant** *peace*.

חִנָּא וְחִסְדָּא וְרַחֲמִין — *Grace, kindness, and mercy.*
[*Emek Brachah* demonstrates that these three words are often used synonymously. Nevertheless, there are differences of meaning between them and, when all three are used together as they are here, we must assume that they are meant as separate and distinct. Some interpretations of the three terms are as follows:]

— There are three stages in the life of man: a period of growth and development; a period of maturity when he capitalizes on the spiritual development of his fruitful years but fails to grow further; and a period of decline. God nourishes him in all three stages, but the degree of Divine compassion varies. During the time of growth, man is nourished by God's חִנָּא, *grace*, for he is worthy of God's gifts. In his period of maturity, he may be unworthy of *grace*, because although his accomplishments are great, he may no longer advance; God then sustains him through חִסְדָּא, *kindness*. Later, when man is in decline and thus undeserving, he is nourished through רַחֲמִין, *God's mercy* (*Ikkarim*).

— The most deserving individuals are nourished through God's חִנָּא, *grace*, while at the other extreme, even the least worthy are still the

מִן קֳדָם אֲבוּהוֹן דִּי בִשְׁמַיָּא (וְאַרְעָא). וְאִמְרוּ
אָמֵן: אמן

יְהֵא שְׁלָמָא רַבָּא מִן שְׁמַיָּא. וְחַיִּים (טוֹבִים).
עָלֵינוּ וְעַל כָּל יִשְׂרָאֵל. וְאִמְרוּ אָמֵן: אמן

עֹשֶׂה שָׁלוֹם (בעשי"ת: הַשָּׁלוֹם) בִּמְרוֹמָיו. הוּא
(בְּרַחֲמָיו) יַעֲשֶׂה שָׁלוֹם עָלֵינוּ וְעַל כָּל יִשְׂרָאֵל.
וְאִמְרוּ אָמֵן: אמן

recipients of רַחֲמִין, *mercy*, by virtue of God's compassion upon every living being. Those in between are provided for through חֶסְדָּא, *kindness* (R' Hirsch).

חֵנָּא, *grace*, is the quality which makes a person beloved by others; חֶסְדָּא, *kindness*, refers to a generous considerate human being who bestows goodness upon others, even when it is apparently unearned; רַחֲמִין, *mercy*, is the quality of compassion by which one withholds punishment even when the deeds of a wrongdoer call for it (*Siach Yitzchak*).

— One who is the recipient of חֵנָּא, *grace*, does have merit and is deserving of generous treatment, but he is given more than he deserves. [See *Berachos* 7a. The gloss to *Tosafos, Rosh HaShanah* 17b applies this term also to one who cannot withstand the temptation to sin, but asks that God prevent him from transgressing.][1] God's חֶסְדָּא, *kindness*, comes into play for one who is entirely undeserving of mercy, but who receives it, thanks to God's limitless kindness. For those who have earned reward for their deeds, God's רַחֲמִין, *mercy*, decrees that they receive more than they have earned (*Emek Brachah*).

The gloss to *Tosafos, Rosh*

1. The *Midrash* [*Shemos Rabbah* 45:6] relates that God showed Moses the treasury of Divine gifts, as it were. Moses asked God to identify each type of gift, to which He responded, 'This treasure is for those who faithfully observe My *mitzvos*. This treasure is for those who raise orphans.'

So it went from chest to chest until Moses came to the largest of all. God explained, 'This treasure chest is reserved for the undeserving. If I desire to assist them חִנָּם, *free*, of any compelling cause, I take a portion from here.'

*Etz Yosef* explains that the chest is so huge because most people do not merit Divine help.

from before their Father *Who is in Heaven*
(and on earth). Now respond: Amen.

Congregation responds: *Amen.*

*May there be abundant peace from Heaven,
and (good) life, upon us and upon all Israel.*
Now respond: Amen.

Congregation responds: *Amen.*

*He Who makes (the) peace in His heights,
may He (in His Mercy) make peace upon us,
and upon all Israel.* Now respond: Amen.

Congregation responds: *Amen.*

HaShanah 17b interprets רַחֲמִים, *mercy*, as God's intervention *before* a sin is committed in order to prevent a person from being placed in a predicament beyond the capacity of his will-power.

*Sforno* interprets this attribute as God's willingness to ease the intensity of the suffering He imposed in punishment for sin.

אֲבוּהוֹן דִי בִשְׁמַיָּא — *Their Father Who is in Heaven.*

This version, following *Rambam* and other texts, is cited by *Avodas Yisrael* as the correct one. Although many *siddurim* add a word: אֲבוּהוֹן דִּי בִשְׁמַיָּא וְאַרְעָא, *their Father Who is* in Heaven **and on earth,** the above commentators agree that such a text is anomalous and clearly in error. God is often described in Rabbinic literature as our Father *in Heaven,* but never as our Father *on earth,* as well. *Abudraham's* text reads מָארֵי שְׁמַיָּא וְאַרְעָא, *Master of Heaven and earth.* Emek Brachah notes that the commonly used version apparently combined the texts of *Rambam* and *Abudraham.*

R' *Yaakov Emden* reads מָרָא שְׁמַיָּא, *Master of Heaven.*

[Continue יְהֵא שְׁלָמָא. For commentary, see stiches 10-11 of the *Full Kaddish.*]

**יִתְגַּדַּל** וְיִתְקַדַּשׁ שְׁמֵהּ רַבָּא. אמן
בְּעָלְמָא דִּי הוּא עָתִיד לְאִתְחַדָּתָּא.
וּלְאַחֲיָאָה מֵתַיָּא. וּלְאַסָּקָא יָתְהוֹן לְחַיֵּי עָלְמָא.
וּלְמִבְנֵא קַרְתָּא דִי יְרוּשְׁלֵם. וּלְשַׁכְלָלָא הֵיכְלֵהּ
בְּגַוַּהּ. וּלְמֶעְקַר פָּלְחָנָא נָכְרָאָה מִן אַרְעָא.

### קַדִּישׁ לְאַחַר הַקְּבוּרָה וּלְסִיּוּם מַסֶּכֶת

## The Kaddish After a Burial and after Completion of a Tractate.

More directly than any other text of *Kaddish*, this *Kaddish* refers to the state of perfection which will come with the Redemption and the End of Days. The first such blessing to be mentioned in this special addition to *Kaddish* is the Divine promise that God will resuscitate the dead who, in life, did not prove to be unworthy. It goes on to list other Divine gifts that will shower upon earth during that period of spiritual beneficence.

According to *Rambam (Nusach HaKaddish)*, it was recited at the conclusion of all Torah study. *Abarbanel* comments that it was recited after burials and on *Tishah B'Av*. *Ramban* ruled that it was to be recited at the burial of תַּלְמִיד דְּרָשָׁן, *a scholar who expounded the Torah (Toras HaAdam)*. The connection between this *Kaddish* and such occasions is obvious. Devotion to the study of Torah is Israel's prime mission and its guarantee of Redemption. A scholar who teaches Torah to the community will surely rise again, and there can be no greater consolation at a burial or on the national day of mourning than to recall God's guarantee that the dead will live again.

Thus, the same *Kaddish* is equally as relevant to the סִיּוּם [*siyum*], *completion* (of a tractate of *Talmud* or an order of *Mishnah*), celebration and to the burial. To the participants in the *siyum*, it proclaims that joyful Redemption is the eventual result of dedication to Torah study; to the mourners who have just parted with a loved one, it proclaims an ebullient expression of confidence that life does not end with the grave.

בְּעָלְמָא דִּי הוּא עָתִיד לְאִתְחַדָּתָּא — *In the world which will be renewed.*

The Sages teach that the universe will cease to exist in its present form and will be renewed in a more exalted spiritual form (*Rosh HaShanah 31a; Sanhedrin 97a*). As we have seen above in the commentary to the standard text of *Kaddish*, the ultimate goal of history is that God's Name be sanctified. This version of *Kaddish* declares that the ultimate sanctification will take place in the world's highest spiritual manifestation (*Abudraham*).

Our reading of this *Kaddish* follows that of *Avodas Yisrael* and, with very slight variations, R' *Yaakov Emden*. In this version, the word לְאִתְחַדָּתָּא, *will be renewed*, is not a transitive verb; the world of the future is described, but we are not told *who* will renew it, although it is obvious, of course, that God will do so. An alternate version refers to God as the subject of the phrase: בְּעָלְמָא דְהוּא עָתִיד לְחַדָּתָא, *in the world* which He [i.e., God] *will renew (Avodas Yisrael)*.

וּלְאַחֲיָאָה מֵתַיָּא — *And where He will resuscitate the dead.*

That the dead will live again in a better world is a principle of our belief (*Abudraham*). It is the last of

# ✑ Kaddish After a Burial and After the Completion of a Tractate

M ay His great Name be exalted and sanctified

Congregation responds: *Amen.*

in the world which will be renewed,
And where He will resuscitate the dead
and raise them up to eternal life,
And rebuild the city of Jerusalem
and complete His Temple within it,
And uproot alien worship from the earth,

*Rambam's Thirteen Principles of Faith*, which are listed in all *siddurim*: 'I believe with a perfect belief that there will be a resuscitation of the dead at the time when the Creator, Blessed be He, so desires, and His remembrance will be exalted forever and ever.'

*Rambam* explains this principle at length in his *Commentary to Mishnah (Sanhedrin* ch. 11).

[This reference to eventual new life for the dead provides the reason this *Kaddish* is recited at burials. Not only is it fundamental to Jewish belief that the dead will be brought back to life, but it is a source of comfort to both the departed and his loved ones that life has a meaning and purpose that survive an essentially temporary death.]

וּלְאַסָקָא יָתְהוֹן לְחַיֵּי עָלְמָא — *And raise them up to eternal life.*

[This reading follows the plain meaning of the Talmud as elucidated by *Ramban* and others, that those who are resurrected following the Redemption will live forever. *Rambam*, however, omits this phrase from the *Kaddish* because he maintains that the resuscitated dead will live normal, though healthier and more fruitful lives, and then

die again — after which their souls will receive their reward in the World to Come. These eschatological opinions are explained briefly by *R' Bachya* to *Deuteronomy* 30:15 and at greater length by *Rambam* in *Maamar T'chiyos HaMeisim* and *Ramban* near the end of *Shaar HaGemul*.]

וּלְמִבְנֵא קַרְתָּא דִי יְרוּשְׁלֵם — *And rebuild the city of Jerusalem.*

[An integral part of the future Redemption and sanctification of the Name is that the Holy City be rebuilt in all its grandeur.]

וּלְשַׁכְלָלָא הֵיכְלֵהּ בְּגַוַּהּ — *And complete His Temple within it.*

[The *Kaddish* goes in an ascending order of holiness: first the city, then the Temple.]

וּלְמֶעְקַר פָּלְחָנָא נֻכְרָאָה מִן אַרְעָא — *And uproot alien worship from the earth.*

This phrase is based on *Zechariah* 13:2 which describes how God will uproot all idols and idolatry after having having established the supremacy of Jerusalem and the ascendancy of the Davidic dynasty (*Abudraham; Avodas Yisrael*).

[As the commentators to *Zechariah* 13:2 explain, the aware-

וְלְאַתָּבָא פָּלְחָנָא דִי שְׁמַיָּא לְאַתְרָהּ. וְיַמְלִיךְ
קוּדְשָׁא בְּרִיךְ הוּא בְּמַלְכוּתֵהּ וִיקָרֵהּ. (וְיַצְמַח
פֻּרְקָנֵהּ וִיקָרֵב מְשִׁיחֵהּ. אמן) בְּחַיֵּיכוֹן וּבְיוֹמֵיכוֹן וּבְחַיֵּי
דְכָל בֵּית יִשְׂרָאֵל. בַּעֲגָלָא וּבִזְמַן קָרִיב.
וְאִמְרוּ אָמֵן: אמן

יְהֵא שְׁמֵהּ רַבָּא מְבָרַךְ לְעָלַם וּלְעָלְמֵי
עָלְמַיָּא:

יִתְבָּרַךְ וְיִשְׁתַּבַּח וְיִתְפָּאַר וְיִתְרוֹמַם וְיִתְנַשֵּׂא
וְיִתְהַדָּר וְיִתְעַלֶּה וְיִתְהַלָּל שְׁמֵהּ דְּקֻדְשָׁא בְּרִיךְ
הוּא. בריך הוא [אמן]

לְעֵלָּא מִן כָּל (בעשי״ת: לְעֵלָּא לְעֵלָּא מִכָּל) בִּרְכָתָא
וְשִׁירָתָא תֻּשְׁבְּחָתָא וְנֶחֱמָתָא. דַּאֲמִירָן בְּעָלְמָא.
וְאִמְרוּ אָמֵן: אמן

[לסיום]

[עַל יִשְׂרָאֵל וְעַל רַבָּנָן. וְעַל תַּלְמִידֵיהוֹן וְעַל כָּל
תַּלְמִידֵי תַלְמִידֵיהוֹן. וְעַל כָּל מָאן דְּעָסְקִין בְּאוֹרַיְתָא.
דִי בְאַתְרָא הָדֵין וְדִי בְכָל אֲתַר וַאֲתַר.
יְהֵא לְהוֹן וּלְכוֹן שְׁלָמָא רַבָּא. חִנָּא וְחִסְדָּא וְרַחֲמִין.
וְחַיִּין אֲרִיכִין. וּמְזוֹנֵי רְוִיחֵי. וּפֻרְקָנָא מִן קֳדָם אֲבוּהוֹן
דִּי בִשְׁמַיָּא (וְאַרְעָא). וְאִמְרוּ אָמֵן: אמן]

יְהֵא שְׁלָמָא רַבָּא מִן שְׁמַיָּא. וְחַיִּים (טוֹבִים).
עָלֵינוּ וְעַל כָּל יִשְׂרָאֵל. וְאִמְרוּ אָמֵן: אמן
עֹשֶׂה שָׁלוֹם (בעשי״ת: הַשָּׁלוֹם) בִּמְרוֹמָיו. הוּא
(בְּרַחֲמָיו) יַעֲשֶׂה שָׁלוֹם עָלֵינוּ וְעַל כָּל יִשְׂרָאֵל.
וְאִמְרוּ אָמֵן: אמן

ness of God's greatness will be so
acute that people will no longer be
led astray by false prophets. Thus,
the implication of the verse is not

that God will actually destroy the
physical remnants of idolatry, but
that the human perception of God's
truth will allow no room for **pagan**

*and return the service of Heaven to its place*
*And where the Holy One, Blessed be He,*
*will reign in His sovereignty and splendor*
(*And cause His salvation to sprout*
*and bring near His Messiah —*     Congregation responds: *Amen.*)

*During your life and during your days*
*and during the lifetime of the entire*
*House of Israel,*
*Swiftly and soon.*     *Now respond: Amen.*

Congregation responds: *Amen.*

Congregation responds aloud with the following stich, and *chazzan* repeats:

*May His great Name be blessed forever and ever.*

*Blessed, lauded, glorified, extolled,*
*upraised, honored, elevated, and praised*
*Be the Name of the Holy One,*
*Blessed be He —*     Congregation responds: *Blessed be He.*

(Some respond: *Amen*).

(During Ten Days of Repentance: *Exceedingly*)

*Beyond all blessings, songs, praises, and consolations*
*that are uttered on earth.*   *Now respond: Amen.*

Congregation responds: *Amen.*

[At a *siyum* add the bracketed stiches; at a burial omit and resume with *May there.*]
[*Upon Israel, upon the teachers,*
*their disciples and all their disciples' disciples,*
*And upon all those who engage in the study of Torah,*
*who are here or anywhere else:*
*May they and you have abundant peace,*
*grace, kindness, and mercy,*
*Long life, ample nourishment, and salvation*
*from before their Father Who is in Heaven (and on earth).*
*Now respond: Amen.*

Congregation responds: *Amen.*]

*May there be abundant peace from Heaven,*
*and (good) life, upon us and upon all Israel.*
*Now respond: Amen.*

Congregation responds: *Amen.*

*He Who makes (the) peace in His heights,*
*may He (in His Mercy) make peace upon us,*
*and upon all Israel.*
*Now respond: Amen*

Congregation responds: *Amen.*

beliefs. This explains why we speak first of rebuilding Jerusalem and the Temple, and only later of destroying idols. If physical destruction were meant, it would have been more logical to destroy the idols before rebuilding the holy places.]

וּלְאָתָבָא פָּלְחָנָא דִי שְׁמַיָּא לְאַתְרֵהּ — And return the service of Heaven to its place.

[When Ramban emigrated to Eretz Yisrael in his old age, he was shocked at the desecration which grew progressively greater as he approached Jerusalem and the site of the Temple. He wrote to his family, 'the holier the place, the greater its degradation.' Thus we look ahead to the time when God will allow us to reverse the process and return His service to the holy places in a progressively greater extent.]

וְיַמְלִיךְ קֻדְשָׁא בְּרִיךְ הוּא בְּמַלְכוּתֵהּ וִיקָרֵהּ — And [where] the Holy One, Blessed be He, will reign in His sovereignty and splendor.

[God's kingdom, in the sense that He is acknowledged by all as Master, is the climax of our longing for sanctification of His Name.]

Continue בְּחַיֵּיכוֹן. For commentary see stich 3 of Kaddish.

עַל יִשְׂרָאֵל — Upon Israel.

This is added only at a סִיוּם, Completion of Tractate or Order of Mishnah. For commentary, see Rabbis' Kaddish.

תם ונשלם שבח לאל בורא עולם

# ❧ Mourner's *Kaddish*

Transliterated with Ashkenazic pronunciation

Yisgadal *v'yiskadash sh'mei rabbaw* (Cong. — *Amein*).
   *B'allmaw dee v'raw chir'usei v'yamlich malchusei,*
[Nusach Sefard — *V'yatzmach purkanei v'kareiv m'shichei*
(Cong. — *Amein*)].
*b'chayeichon, uv'yomeichon, uv'chayei d'chol beis yisroel,*
*ba'agawlaw u'vizman kawriv, v'imru: Amein.*
(Cong. — *Amein. Y'hei sh'mei rabbaw m'vawrach*
*l'allam u'l'allmei allmayaw.*)

*Y'hei sh'mei rabbaw m'vawrach, l'allam u'l'allmei allmayaw.*
*Yis'bawrach, v'yishtabach, v'yispaw'ar, v'yisromam, v'yis'nassei,*
*v'yis'hadaw, v'yis'aleh, v'yis'halawl*
*sh'mei d'kudshaw b'rich hu* (Cong. — *b'rich hu*).
*L'aylaw min kol*
[From Rosh Hashanah to Yom Kippur substitute: *L'aylaw ul'aylaw mikol*]
*bir'chawsaw v'shirawsaw,*
*tush'b'chawsaw v'nechemawsaw,*
*da'ami'rawn b'allmaw, v'imru: Amein* (Cong. — *Amein*).

*Y'hei shlawmaw rabbaw min sh'mayaw,*
*v'chayim* [Nusach Sefard — *tovim*] *awleinu v'al kol yisroel,*
*v'imru: Amein* (Cong. — *Amein*).

Take three steps back, bow left and say, 'Oseh. . .';
   bow right and say, 'hu b'rachamawv ya'aseh. . .';
bow forward and say, 'v'al kol yisroel v'imru: Amein.'

*Oseh shawlom bim'ro'mawv,*
*hu ya'aseh shawlom awleinu,*
*v'al kol yisroel v'imru: Amein* (Cong. — *Amein*).

Remain standing in place for a few moments, then take three steps forward.

# Rabbis' Kaddish/*Kaddish D'Rabbanan*

Yisgadal v'yiskadash sh'mei rabbaw (Cong. — Amein).
 B'allmaw dee v'raw chir'usei v'yamlich malchusei,
[Nusach Sefard — V'yatzmach purkanei v'kareiv m'shichei
(Cong. — Amein)].
b'chayeichon, uv'yomeichon, uv'chayei d'chol beis yisroel,
ba'agawlaw u'vizman kawriv, v'imru: Amein.
(Cong. — Amein. Y'hei sh'mei rabbaw m'vawrach
l'allam u'l'allmei allmayaw.)

 Y'hei sh'mei rabbaw m'vawrach, l'allam u'l'allmei allmayaw.
Yis'bawrach, v'yishtabach, v'yispaw'ar, v'yisromam, v'yis'nassei,
v'yis'hadaw, v'yis'aleh, v'yis'halawl
sh'mei d'kudshaw b'rich hu (Cong. — b'rich hu).
L'aylaw min kol

[From Rosh Hashanah to Yom Kippur substitute: L'aylaw ul'aylaw mikol]
bir'chawsaw v'shirawsaw,
tush'b'chawsaw v'nechemawsaw,
da'ami'rawn b'allmaw, v'imru: Amein (Cong. — Amein).

Al yisroel v'al rabaw'nawn v'al talmidei'hon,
v'al kol talmidei salmidei'hon, v'al kol mawn d'awskin b'oray'saw,
dee v'as'raw haw'dain, v'dee b'chol asar va'asar.
Y'hei l'hon u'l'chon shlaw'maw rabbaw,
chee'naw v'chisdaw v'rachamin,
v'chayin arichin, u'm'zonei r'vichei, u'furkawnaw
min kaw'dawm a'vu'hone dee vi'sh'ma'yaw [Nusach Sefard — v'araw]
v'imru: Amein (Cong. — Amein).

Y'hei shlawmaw rabbaw min sh'mayaw,
v'chayim [Nusach Sefard — tovim] awleinu v'al kol yisroel,
v'imru: Amein (Cong. — Amein).

Take three steps back, bow left and say, 'Oseh...';
bow right and say, 'hu b'rachamawv ya'aseh...';
bow forward and say, 'v'al kol yisroel v'imru: Amein.'

Oseh shawlom bim'ro'mawv,
hu b'rachamawv ya'aseh shawlom awleinu,
v'al kol yisroel v'imru: Amein (Cong. — Amein).

Remain standing in place for a few moments, then take three steps forward.

# ◆§ Kaddish HaGadol/Kaddish After Burial

Transliterated with Ashkenazic pronunciation

Yisgadal v'yiskadash sh'mei rabbaw (Cong. – Amein).
 B'allmaw dee hu awsid l'ischadawsaw,
u'l'achayawsaw meisayaw,
u'l'asawkaw yaws'hon l'chayei allmaw,
u'l'mivnei kartaw dee yerushleim,
u'l'shachlawlaw heichlei b'gavaw,
u'l'me'kar paelchawnaw nuchraw'aw min ar'aw,
u'l'asawvaw pawlchawnaw dee sh'mayaw l'asrei,
v'yamlich kudshaw b'rich hu b'malchusei veekawrei,
[Nusach Sefard – V'yatzmach purkanei v'kareiv m'shichei
(Cong. – Amein)].
b'chayeichon, uv'yomeichon, uv'chayei d'chol beis yisroel,
ba'agawlaw u'vizman kawriv, v'imru: Amein.
(Cong. – Amein. Y'hei sh'mei rabbaw m'vawrach l'allam u'l'allme
allmayaw.)

Y'hei sh'mei rabbaw m'vawrach, l'allam u'l'allmei allmayaw.
Yis'bawrach, v'yishtabach, v'yispaw'ar, v'yisromam, v'yis'nassei,
v'yis'hadaw, v'yis'aleh, v'yis'halawl
sh'mei d'kudshaw b'rich hu (Cong. – b'rich hu).
L'aylaw min kol
[From Rosh Hashanah to Yom Kippur substitute: L'aylaw ul'aylaw mikol]
bir'chawsaw v'shirawsaw,
tush'b'chawsaw v'nechemawsaw,
da'ami'rawn b'allmaw, v'imru: Amein (Cong. – Amein).

Y'hei shlawmaw rabbaw min sh'mayaw,
v'chayim [Nusach Sefard – tovim] awleinu v'al kol yisroel,
v'imru: Amein (Cong. – Amein).

Take three steps back, bow left and say, 'Oseh. . .';
bow right and say, 'hu b'rachamawv ya'aseh. . .';
bow forward and say, 'v'al kol yisroel v'imru: Amein.'

Oseh shawlom bim'ro'mawv,
hu ya'aseh shawlom awleinu,
v'al kol yisroel v'imru: Amein (Cong. – Amein).

Remain standing in place for a few moments, then take three steps forward.

This volume is part of
THE ARTSCROLL SERIES®
an ongoing project of
translations, commentaries and expositions
on Scripture, Mishnah, Talmud, Halachah,
liturgy, history, the classic Rabbinic writings,
biographies, and thought.

For a brochure of current publications
visit your local Hebrew bookseller
or contact the publisher:

Mesorah Publications, ltd

4401 Second Avenue
Brooklyn, New York 11232
(718) 921-9000